theinsurancebook

what Canadians really need to know before buying insurance

Sally Praskey

Helena Moncrieff

Prentice Hall Canada

Canadian Cataloguing in Publication Data

Praskey, Sally
    The insurance book
ISBN 0-13-012274-2

1. Insurance. I. Moncrieff, Helena, II. Title
HG8051.P72   1999   368   C98-933067-2

© 1999 Sally Praskey and Helena Moncrieff
Prentice-Hall Canada Inc., Scarborough, Ontario
Pearson Education

Prentice-Hall, Inc., Upper Saddle River, New Jersey
Prentice-Hall International (UK) Limited, London
Prentice-Hall of Australia, Pty. Limited, Sydney
Prentice-Hall Hispanoamericana, S.A., Mexico City
Prentice-Hall of India Private Limited, New Delhi
Prentice-Hall of Japan, Inc., Tokyo
Simon & Schuster Southeast Asia Private Limited, Singapore
Editora Prentice-Hall do Brasil, Ltda., Rio de Janeiro

ISBN 0-13-012274-2

Editorial Director, Trade Group: Andrea Crozier
Copy Editor: Liba Berry
Production Editor: Alex Moore
Production Coordinator: Barb Ollerenshaw
Art Direction: Mary Opper
Cover and Interior Design: Victoria Primicias / Pure
Page Layout: Gail Ferreira Ng-A-Kien

1 2 3 4 5   03 02 01 00 99

Printed and bound in Canada

Visit the Prentice Hall Canada Web site! Send us your comments, browse our catalogues, and more. www.phcanada.com

This publication contains the opinions and ideas of its authors and is designed to provide useful advice in regard to the subject matter covered. The authors and publisher are not engaged in rendering legal, accounting, or other professional services in this publication. This publication is not intended to provide a basis for action in particular circumstances without consideration by a competent professional. The authors, publisher, and all others directly or indirectly involved with this publication expressly disclaim any responsibility for any liability, loss, or risk, personal or otherwise, which is incurred as a consequence, directly or indirectly, of the use and application of any of the contents of this book.

The Consumers Council of Canada is pleased to see this information published but can make no claim as to its validity.

contents

acknowledgments

The authors gratefully acknowledge the generous assistance of the following people and organizations in the writing of this book:

Helen Anderson, Consumers' Association of Canada
Canadian Life and Health Insurance Association of Canada
Bruce Caplan, Sun Life
CIBC Insurance
Consumers Council of Canada
Insurance Canada
Insurance Council of Canada
Michael Maclean, President, I.C.T. Insurance Consulting and Training Inc.
Judy Moncrieff, Focus Group

foreword

by the Consumers Council of Canada

In today's hectic and complex world, it is increasingly difficult for consumers to feel that they are making the right choices when they buy insurance. Like the world we live in, insurance has become increasingly complex.

With this in mind, the Consumers Council of Canada supports this book in providing consumers with useful information about home, automobile, life, health, disability, and travel insurance. *The Insurance Book* is a credible, independent source that will help consumers make the right insurance purchases; the book's comprehensive lists of Frequently Asked Questions will ensure that consumers make astute decisions about buying insurance, as will the clear and concise explanatory sections.

Introduction

Every year, many of us spend hundreds—if not thousands—of dollars on insurance, be it for health, life, home, car, travel or other. Yet few of us know exactly what we have bought—and, perhaps even more importantly, *not* bought—until we find ourselves in the unfortunate position of suffering a loss that triggers an insurance claim. If we haven't taken the time up front to find out what our insurance does—and doesn't—cover, we could be in for a nasty surprise come claims time.

Having worked with both insurance companies and insurance consumers, we were struck by how often the two groups fail to connect—because of different expectations, lack of understanding of each other's knowledge base, or simply because of language that means something different to each party.

This book is intended to help eliminate unpleasant surprises by arming you with the information you need to make sure you get the right coverage at the best price. Despite what some insurance providers might have you believe, insurance can be a complex purchase that is further complicated by jargon and practices that may not be communicated clearly to consumers. Many consumers simply don't know what they don't know, and so cannot ask the appropriate questions about their insurance.

Who should read this book? Just about anyone—from the newly-licensed teen in search of insurance for a first car to snowbirds heading south and seeking health coverage. Throughout the book, we refer to various lifestyle situations and suggest how these could affect the type of coverage you might require. After all, your insurance needs will change according to your age and lifestyle, but your need for insurance will not.

To allow you to access information quickly and easily, we've organized the book in a question-and-answer format, with different chapters devoted to different kinds of insurance. Depending on your needs, you can refer to specific questions or read the book chapter by chapter. The first chapter introduces you to some of the basics about insurance; each subsequent chapter features an introduction explaining why you might want or need that particular kind of coverage. At the end of every chapter we supply a chapter-specific glossary of "keywords" and a checklist of essential questions to ask your insurance provider.

The appendices feature a glossary of insurance terms and a resource list of insurance-related organizations that you can contact for further information and assistance. Interspersed throughout the chapters are tips, cautions, scenarios, and even some real-life insurance humour—yes, there *is* a lighter side to insurance!

We know that researching and shopping for insurance is not high on most people's list of favourite activities. But if you ever suffer a serious loss —and we hope you don't—it will have been time well-spent. We believe this book will make the process of understanding and buying insurance easier.

Sally Praskey
Helena Moncrieff

why insurance?

Who needs insurance

How insurance works

How insurance is sold

Insurance terminology

How insurers price policies

Insurance: Who Needs It—And When?

WHEN IT COMES TO YOUR LIST OF INTERESTING SUBJECTS, insurance probably ranks right up there with "101 creative uses for polyester." But the truth is, we all rely on insurance—just as we do polyester!—throughout our lives. Whether you've just passed your driver's test, moved into your own apartment, left home to attend college, bought a house, started a family, launched your own business from home, or made plans to travel outside Canada, you need insurance. Insurance protects you and your family, as well as your home and belongings. Without insurance, the economy would practically come to a standstill, because starting and operating any kind of business would be too risky—one fire and your livelihood would go up in smoke. In fact, you couldn't even drive a car, because a serious accident would wipe out all your savings. Nor could you borrow money to buy a house, as no lending institution would allow you to mortgage a property that wasn't insured.

Canadians spend almost $50 billion on insurance annually, according to combined statistics from the Insurance Bureau of Canada and the Canadian Life and Health Insurance Association. Many of us fork out thousands of dollars each year on insurance—it's the fifth-largest expenditure a family makes, according to 1996 Statistics Canada figures—but the strange thing is, few of us know what we've bought until we need it. Then we sometimes get a nasty surprise when we find out our insurance doesn't cover a particular loss. Perhaps our agent or broker didn't explain what our policy did *and didn't* cover when we bought it; likely we didn't read the policy ourselves—who does? But now it's too late—it's all water under the bridge—or in your basement!—and you simply have to grit your teeth and foot the repair bill.

Imagine spending the same amount on, say, a new high-tech sound system as you do on your insurance. You'd certainly want to make sure you were getting good value for your hard-earned cash, and you'd probably spend a lot more time shopping around for the sound equipment than for your insurance. Let's face it—it's pretty hard to get excited about buying a new insurance policy!

You'd also want to replace your sound system when it became old or outdated (which doesn't take long these days). Similarly, your insurance needs

As inevitable as death and taxes...

Insurance was just as important back in 1940, as the then-editor of Canadian Insurance magazine, a national trade publication founded in 1905, pointed out in an editorial.

"...Insurance, like the atmosphere, is all around us. We doubt if there is any person in Canada who has been able to avoid its influence. The majority of us have been under the protection of several kinds of insurance, without even realizing that fact. Our education has been made possible by it. The buildings in which we were born and the school house in which we were educated had many kinds of insurance on it; the clothes we wear, the seats on which we sit, the books we read, the pens and pencils we use, the electric light; everything about us has had insurance of several kinds associated with it. It is like death and taxes; it cannot be avoided..."

will change through various stages of life, as well as with changes in job status. For example, a single person starting a career probably will not need life insurance just yet, since he or she doesn't have a family to protect; empty nesters moving into a condominium will need different insurance than a homeowner; self-employed people may need health coverage that others usually get through their workplace, and so on.

Many factors affect an individual's insurance—age, marital and familial status, employment status, the purchase of a new car or new home, and the acquisition of valuables, like jewellery, a state-of-the-art computer, or even a rare comic book. This book is intended to prevent that nasty surprise at claims time, by telling you what *isn't* covered in most policies, and how to get the right coverage at the best price.

Spreading the risk—How insurance works

While it sometimes seems that insurance companies work in mysterious ways, the idea behind insurance is simple: it uses the payments of many to cover the losses of a few. The money you pay for your insurance—your premiums—goes into one large pool at the insurance company. Those of us who suffer a loss that is insured can then draw from that pool. Because only a few of us need to draw from the pool in any given year, there is enough money in it to pay major losses like those incurred as a result of fire or a serious automobile accident. This concept is called spreading the risk, or risk sharing.

However, the pool must be replenished, or refilled, each year, so it will hold enough money to cover the coming year's losses. You can imagine how quickly it can be drained by one major disaster. The 1998 Quebec ice storm alone resulted in an estimated 700,000 claims for damage totalling $1.14 billion, according to the Insurance Bureau of Canada. That's enough to suck the pool, if not dry, at least to ankle depth. In fact, many insurance companies do not even make a profit on the premiums they receive as compared with the money they pay out in claims and spend to operate the business. Rather, their profit derives from their investments.

Your insurance policy represents a promise to protect you against certain "perils"—or causes of loss—for a given period of time, usually a year. This promise is renewed on a year-by-year basis; your premiums do not "build up" for you to draw upon when needed (except in the case of certain life insurance products—whole life, for example—that are designed with an investment component). In fact, this is one of the most common misconceptions about insurance. Consumers complain that they faithfully pay their premiums year after year. Yet, when they finally need their insurance to cover a small loss, they can't make a claim, because the cost of paying the deductible (the portion of the claim that *you* have to pay) may be as high as, or even higher than, the amount of the claim itself. Then there's always the risk—there's that word again!—of premiums going up as the result of a claim, even a small one. It's a familiar, and understandable, litany.

Another common misconception is that insurance covers every misfortune that might befall you. If that were the case, no one could afford the premiums. Neither is insurance intended to be a maintenance policy, so don't even think of contacting your insurer if your aging roof leaks and damages your broadloom, or your sofa gets ratty from wear and tear. Nor is it intended to cover minor losses that consumers could afford to pay for themselves. Rather, insurance is intended primarily to protect you against serious, and unforeseen, loss or injury that you could not pay for otherwise: for example, a major car accident, a fire that destroys your home, the theft of your precious jewellery, the death of a spouse and the consequent loss of that individual's income. It is not designed to replace your $200 lost sweater, as inconvenient and annoying as that loss may be. If insurers were to pay all of these smaller claims, there would not be enough money left in the pool to pay the large ones. If you ever suffer a major loss, you will soon realize that that's when insurance really pays its way.

Many consumer complaints stem from a lack of understanding of how insurance works and what it is designed to cover. The insurance industry, for the most part, has failed to communicate this information to consumers, although a number of initiatives are now in place to rectify this shortcoming.

In the beginning…

When businessmen congregated in Edward Lloyd's coffee house back in 17th century London, England, to catch up on the latest shipping news, little did they suspect their impromptu coffee klatches would spawn the granddaddy of all insurers, Lloyd's of London (now known simply as Lloyd's). Although merchants had been insuring ships and cargoes since the 15th century, insurance companies did not yet exist. Marine insurance was supplied by private individuals on an informal basis as a sideline to their normal businesses.

That all changed in the 17th century, when "brokers" began to take the policy around to wealthy merchants who would agree to pay a portion of the claim if the ship went down. Those who accepted a share of the risk signed their names with the amount, one beneath the other, at the bottom of the policy wording. Hence the term "underwriters," which is still used today to describe those at insurance companies who decide whether or not to accept a certain risk, and, if so, what price to charge for it.

From its humble beginnings in the coffee house, Lloyd's branched out into other types of insurance, and made its mark insuring unusual risks, like 1940s movie star Betty Grable's famous million-dollar legs.

Although Lloyd's is commonly accepted as the first formal insurance company, historians believe the concept of insurance was practised as early as 5000 B.C. in China. As merchants sailing on the treacherous Yangtze River approached rapids, they would redistribute their cargoes to several ships. That way, if one went down, no one would lose all their goods. Thus was born the idea of risk sharing—many sharing the losses of a few.

It's a good bet that the first English-language marine policy ever issued had a Canadian connection, as it concerned Newfoundland fish. It was dated October 3, 1604, and read, in part: "In the name of God, Amen. Be it known unto all men by these presents that A.J. of London, Merchant and company, do make assurance and cause themselves and everything of them to be assured, lost, known or not known, from the New Found Land to Toulon and Marseilles upon fish already laden, in the good ship called the Hopewell of London in the burthen of 120 tons or thereabouts..." Some would argue that insurance policies today are just as difficult to understand, despite attempts by insurers to use "plain language."

The first general insurance company operating in Canada was London, England-based Phoenix Assurance Company Limited, which began writing business here in 1804. The first completely Canadian company was the Fire Association of Halifax—now the Halifax Insurance Company—which was established in 1809. Not too long after that, Canada's first prime minister, Sir John A. Macdonald, joined the ranks of insurers. From 1887 to 1891, he was the first president of Dominion of Canada General Insurance, a company that is still going strong today.

What's your line?

Nowadays, there are some 300 insurance companies operating in Canada selling many different kinds, or "lines," of insurance. Generally, most companies sell either "property and casualty" insurance (also referred to as "general" insurance) or "life and health" insurance, but seldom both.

Property and casualty insurance includes automobile insurance, property insurance (insurance for homeowners, condominium owners, and tenants), as well as a variety of commercial and business insurance. An important component of all of the property and casualty lines is liability insurance, which provides protection for an insured person who accidentally injures someone or damages someone else's property and is legally bound to pay for the damage.

Life and health insurance is primarily the bailiwick of the more than 100 life insurance companies operating in Canada, both domestic and foreign-owned. Life insurance provides funds to a designated beneficiary in the event of the policyholder's death. Some of the more common life insurance products include term, universal, and whole life insurance. Health insurance protects against financial loss due to illness, injury, or medical bills, and extends coverage, through a variety of products, beyond that offered by government medicare plans. In fact, medicare itself is a form of insurance, paid for by our tax dollars. Another aspect of health insurance, disability insurance, pays for income lost due to a disabling injury or illness. Often, life, health, travel medical, and disability insurance is provided through employers, but it can also be purchased by individuals. Without health insurance, we'd probably be afraid to set foot outside our homes, let alone play sports or participate in any other activities. Even one broken leg could eat a big chunk out of our savings.

How it's sold

It may seem that everywhere you turn these days, someone, somewhere, is hawking some kind of insurance, whether it be through television, over the Internet, on the phone, through the mail, or plastered on billboards. However, there are actually only four main channels through which insurance is sold. While any of the following could meet your needs, you should choose the one that is convenient for you and with which you are most comfortable. Throughout this book, we use the general term "insurance provider," so as not to favour any one of these channels over another.

Brokers—An insurance broker sells the products of several different insurance companies, and can therefore offer a variety of choices. However, no one broker represents all the companies, so if you want a wide range of quotations, you should consult more than one broker, and ask which companies each one represents. Some brokers are licensed to sell both property/casualty and life/health insurance products, while others sell only one of these two main types of insurance.

Agents—An agent represents only the products of one insurance company. Companies that use their own "captive" agents to sell their products are called "direct insurers." While an agent may not be able to provide you with access to as many products as a broker could, most direct insurers offer a wide enough range to meet the needs of most consumers, at a competitive price.

Direct sellers—Also called "direct-response insurers," these are the newest kids on the block. Like direct insurers who operate through local agents, direct sellers generally sell only the products of their particular company. However, what distinguishes them from direct insurers is that their products are sold via telephone from a central location known as a "call centre," rather than through local agents.

Group plans—Although any of the above channels may supply group insurance, consumers buy it through their workplace, alumni association, professional association, or other group affiliations. Group insurance is generally less expensive for both the insurer and the consumer, because it is sold in quantity to a relatively homogeneous group.

Many brokers, direct insurers, and direct sellers are now promoting insurance over the Internet, offering quotations and, in some cases, even selling insurance online. While this is a convenient service that will no doubt continue to increase in popularity, the watchword for consumers should be "buyer beware." As you will learn from the chapters that follow, there are many options when it comes to buying insurance. The key is to get the right coverage at the best price. When shopping for insurance over the Internet, make sure you're comparing apples with apples. All policies are not alike, and the lowest price may not be the best coverage for you. It's important to ask the right questions before you buy your insurance (see the checklist at the end of each chapter), or you could be left high and dry at claims time.

Speaking of insurance...

"Insurance-speak" is a language unto itself, so it's no wonder consumers get confused trying to decipher their insurance policy. As a first step, get comfortable with the following basic terms that are used throughout the book. Other definitions are listed in the glossary at the back of the book, and at the end of each chapter.

Claim—a person's request for payment by an insurer for a loss covered by a policy. Claims to your own company are called "first-party claims"; claims made by one person against another person's company are known as "third-party claims."

Deductible—nothing to do with income tax, this is the portion of the loss that you agree to pay out of your own pocket, before the insurance company pays the amount that it is obligated to cover. The deductible is subtracted from the total amount paid by your insurer. Therefore, if your claim is for $2,000 and your deductible is $500, you will pay $500 and the insurer will pay $1,500.

Exclusion—specific conditions or circumstances listed in the policy that are not covered by the policy. For example, damage caused by rodents is excluded from your homeowners policy, meaning it is not covered and the insurer will not pay if a squirrel wreaks havoc in your house.

Liability—a legally enforceable financial obligation. Liability insurance pays the losses of other people when you are legally responsible for an accident in which you have injured another person or damaged that individual's property.

Occurrence—an accident that results in bodily injury or property damage during the period of an insurance policy.

Peril—the cause of loss or damage. Your homeowners policy, for example, insures you against perils like windstorm, fire, and theft, among others.

Personal lines insurance—insurance (like homeowners or automobile) for individuals, as opposed to commercial lines insurance, for businesses.

Policy—the legal document issued by the insurance company that outlines the terms and conditions of the insurance.

Policyholder—the person who buys the insurance; also called the "insured."

Premium—the payment required to keep your insurance policy in force.

Risk—the chance of a loss. You insure your house, for example, against the risk of fire.

Underwriting—the process of selecting risks for insurance, and determining how much to charge to insure these risks and which coverage to provide.

Who's who?

It also helps to know the players, so here's a brief primer to help you understand who does what in an insurance company and brokerage.

Actuary—an employee of the insurance company who prices future risks by applying mathematical models to problems of insurance and finance; in other words, develops models to evaluate the financial implications of uncertain future events.

Adjuster—a person who investigates and settles claims on behalf of the insurance company. The adjuster may be either an employee of the company or an independent contractor hired by the company. Less common are public adjusters, who represent the interests of the homeowner or business owner following a property loss, and are paid a percentage of the insurance settlement by the consumer.

Claims handler/examiner—an employee of the insurance company who looks after your claim. This person is supervised by a claims manager.

Customer service representative (CSR)—an employee of the insurance brokerage or company who assists in handling requests from clients and other duties that must be performed. This person is not the same as an insurance broker, who must be licensed.

Underwriter—an employee of the insurance company who decides whether or not the company should accept a particular risk; for example, your house or your life insurance application. The term "underwriter" can also refer to the company. For example: "Company XYZ is the underwriter of that insurance policy."

Pricing your policy

How do insurers decide what to charge for your insurance? It's all based on something called "risk factors." The more risk involved in insuring you, the more you will pay for your insurance. That's where underwriters come in. They decide on what terms to accept a risk, and then price it accordingly. For example, why might you pay more for life insurance than your next-door neighbour, even though you have purchased the same kind of policy? There could be several reasons: perhaps you are a smoker and your neighbour is not; perhaps your occupation is considered more dangerous than your neighbour's (you're a stunt pilot, for example); maybe you like to indulge in what is considered a risky hobby, like skydiving; or perhaps you are much older than your neighbour, or your health is not as good. All of these are risk factors.

The same principle applies to your property. You may discover you're paying more for your home insurance than your neighbour, even though you have the same kind of policy from the same company. Again, there's a logical explanation. Perhaps you rent out the basement of your house, while your neighbour does not; maybe your house is larger in square footage than your neighbour's; or you have some valuable jewellery listed on your policy that your neighbour does not. And so on.

When it comes to home insurance, underwriters price a house according to several risk factors: whether it's occupied by the owner or by tenants; whether it's a single-family dwelling or has multiple tenants; the size and style of the house; and its location (how far it is from a hydrant and fire hall, for example). That's why your country retreat might cost more to insure than your suburban bungalow. Generally, insurance is cheapest on an owner-occupied single-family dwelling, because it is considered a better risk.

In underwriting personal insurance, like property and automobile, the company has already decided what rules it will use to determine if an applicant is eligible for insurance. A risk either fits the company's criteria or it doesn't. If your particular risk doesn't qualify, you will have to modify it to meet the insurer's standards, or shop elsewhere for your insurance, and probably pay a bundle for it.

Life insurance works in a similar way. You will be asked a number of questions on your application to determine your risk status. Risk factors for life insurance include: your age, whether you smoke, your medical history, and your occupation (just how risky is it?). If the company decides you are an acceptable risk, it will agree to insure you. If not, it will refuse the risk, or will charge more to insure you.

There are certain risks that no insurer will agree to cover, because the odds are too great that a loss will occur; for example, a river overflowing and flooding your home, or a volcano erupting and destroying property. Likewise, you may not be able to buy certain types of travel medical or health insurance if you have what is called a "pre-existing condition"—an existing or previous illness that the insurer believes is likely to worsen or recur.

Take a tip

While no one looks forward to buying or renewing their insurance, here are some tips that will make the process a little easier. (These suggestions are discussed in more detail in the chapters that follow.)

- Ask your insurance provider what the policy *doesn't* cover. The perils that are not covered are called "exclusions," and every policy has them. Find out what they are *now*, rather than at claims time. They are listed on your insurance policy, but how many of us bother to read *that?* That's what we thought! Therefore, ask your insurance provider to explain the exclusions before you buy the policy. That's what the insurance provider is paid to do. In the case of life insurance, ask about guaranteed highest and lowest premiums, history of price increases, and interest rate assumptions (see chapter 4 for more details).

- Generally, you get what you pay for. If you're shopping around, make sure you're always comparing apples with apples—not all insurance policies are alike. And, while minor price variation among companies offering similar kinds of coverage is likely, if one insurer is charging *substantially* less, beware. It may not be the ideal company to deal with at claims time.

- Don't cancel your policy by not paying your premium. You will be considered a "bad risk" for default of payment, and charged a higher rate. If you decide not to renew your insurance, notify the insurer in writing.

- Don't switch insurance providers before your policy comes up for renewal, as you will usually have to pay a penalty for cancelling your coverage prematurely. The amount of the penalty will vary depending on how many months are left on your policy when you cancel it. The more months remaining, the higher the penalty.

- Don't switch insurance companies too frequently. For all its sophisticated technology, insurance remains a matter of trust and good faith. Therefore, insurers are not inclined to give the benefit of the doubt to those they do not know. If, on the other hand, you have established a good record with one company, it should stand you in good stead at claims time, or at least put you on firmer ground.

- Don't sweat the small stuff. In the case of home and automobile insurance, that means don't make too many small claims, because each one goes on your record, regardless of the size. Too many claims, even if they weren't all your fault, could result in non-renewal of your coverage.

- Review your insurance needs on a yearly basis. Your circumstances may have changed during the year, and some of these changes should be reflected in your insurance coverage. Don't wait for your insurance provider to ask—most don't.

- Don't intentionally, or even unintentionally, "omit" any details on your insurance application. For instance, if you tell your life insurer that you're a non-smoker, even smoking a few cigarettes a month could result in cancellation of your policy or, worse, denial of a claim. The same holds true if you don't come clean about a pre-existing condition on your travel insurance application. Likewise for automobile or property insurance. Insurers have access to several databases that they can use to check up on your driving and claims history, even if you move to another province, so honesty is the best policy.
- Take steps to prevent losses from occurring in the first place. This is called "risk management." It could be something as simple as installing deadbolt locks on your door to prevent burglaries, in the case of home insurance; or purchasing a car equipped with the latest safety and anti-theft devices. The more measures you take to protect yourself and your property, the less you will have to rely on your insurance, and the less it will cost you in the long run.

Who ya gonna call?

You have a claim that you thought would be covered by your insurance. That's why you bought your policy in the first place, right? Yet your insurance provider is insisting that your claim is not covered under your policy. What do you do?

First, ask your insurance provider to show you exactly where in the policy it states that this particular peril is not covered. It may be that once you have read your policy, you will realize that you have no argument. (That's why it's so important to ask your insurance provider what is *not* covered before you buy your policy.)

However, many claims are not so cut-and-dried. Perhaps, having checked your policy, you still disagree with the insurer's decision. Try to resolve your problem within the company first. Discuss your case with a senior official in the claims department, the claims manager, if possible. This official may make an allowance if there is a grey area, and particularly if you are a good long-term customer. But don't count on it.

If you're still not satisfied, find out if the insurance company (not the broker) has an ombudsperson or an employee who deals with consumer complaints. If so, contact that person.

Another option is to speak with one of the information officers at the consumer assistance centres operated by the Insurance Bureau of Canada (for property and casualty insurance) and the Canadian Life and Health Insurance Association (for life and health insurance questions). (See "Consumer Resources" in Appendix A for the toll-free number for each organization.) While they do not have the authority to intervene in the company's decision, they will advise you as to your best course of action, or tell you if you have a case at all.

Failing that, you can take your case to the insurance ombudsperson (or the department that handles consumer complaints) at the insurance regulator in your province or territory (see "Consumer Resources" in Appendix A). Submit your complaint in writing and support it with the appropriate documentation. Procedures may vary from one area to another, and the decision is not binding.

In the case of property-claim disputes, you could also retain a public adjuster, a licensed adjuster who acts on your behalf to settle your loss with the insurance company, taking a percentage of the final settlement as payment. While public adjusters are not as common in Canada as they are in the United States, and the insurance industry—not surprisingly!—tends to shun them, they represent yet another avenue for dissatisfied consumers.

Finally, you may have to resort to legal action. If you retain a lawyer, choose one who specializes in insurance litigation, and ask in advance about fees. Lawyers' fees for bodily-injury lawsuits are usually payable upon settlement of the case, rather than on an hourly basis.

Most insurance disputes arise from a lack of communication upfront, when the insurance was purchased. Who can blame consumers for crying foul when, for example, they are penalized for small claims that they probably wouldn't have made had they known the surreptitious rules by which insurers play. It's the responsibility of the insurance provider, not only to explain these practices, but to inform the consumer what is, and *isn't*, covered in the policy. Simply handing over a brochure to the consumer will not do the trick. But policyholders must also learn to ask the right questions and make the effort to understand what they are buying. If your insurance provider is not willing to take the time to assess your needs, answer your questions, and explain your policy to you, find one who will. Ask trusted friends or relatives for recommendations, especially if they have experienced a recent claim. Insurance is a big expenditure, and you need to be sure you are getting what you're paying for—the peace of mind that comes from knowing you have the right insurance protection.

Protection for policyholders

OK, you've bought insurance to protect yourself and your belongings, but who protects you if your insurer goes out of business? Although this is an unlikely possibility, the well-publicized collapse of Confederation Life several years ago served as a harsh reminder that it can and does happen. But not to worry. The property and casualty insurance companies and the life and health insurance companies each have funds to protect policyholders in the event of insolvency.

If a property/casualty company were to go bankrupt, the Property and Casualty Insurance Compensation Corporation (PACICC) would come to the rescue. This protection is automatic to policyholders; they don't have to apply for it. There are limits on claims payouts, however. PACICC will pay up to a maximum of $250,000 for unpaid claims for losses arising from a single occurrence. If your claim exceeds $250,000, you may eventually be reimbursed for all or part of the shortfall from funds released by the liquidator. PACICC will also refund 70 per cent of the unexpired portion of your premium to a maximum payout of $700 per policy, applicable from the date of the insurer's collapse.

Life and health insurance company insolvencies are covered by a similar fund, called CompCorp, which stands for Canadian Life and Health Insurance Compensation Corporation. Founded in 1990, CompCorp protects, within limits, Canadian policyholders against loss of benefits or unpaid claims under their life, annuity, and accident and sickness contracts, should a CompCorp member company collapse (see chapter 4 for more details). Neither CompCorp nor PACICC receives any financial support from government; they are funded through assessments and loans from member companies.

The insurance business in Canada is supervised by both federal and provincial governments, but the federal Office of the Superintendent of Financial Institutions oversees the solvency and stability of insurance companies.

Insurance fraud: We all pay

Many of us think that when people cheat on their insurance, it's only the big, rich insurance companies who pay. In fact, we all do, in the form of higher premiums to make up for the lost money. Insurance fraud costs as much as $1.3 billion each year in the property and casualty sector alone, as estimated by the Canadian Coalition Against Insurance Fraud. That means 10 to 15 cents of every dollar you pay for insurance goes to pay false claims.

Falsifying information on an application for an insurance policy is a crime; so is cheating on an insurance claim, or exaggerating a claim. In other words, if you have a legitimate claim, but you decide to embellish it to "make up" for all those premiums you've been paying all those years, you'd be committing insurance fraud.

Insurers have become increasingly vigilant about cracking down on fraudsters, and have put a number of initiatives in place to do so. One of these is a partnership with Crime Stoppers, an international non-profit civilian program that assists police in solving crimes through tips reported by citizens. If the tip leads to a successful resolution of the crime, the person who reported the information is usually eligible for a cash award. All calls are anonymous, and tipsters can collect their rewards without revealing their identity at any point.

If you have information about an insurance fraud, call Crime Stoppers at (800) 222-TIPS. And see "Consumer Resources" in Appendix A for contact information for the Canadian Coalition Against Insurance Fraud.

property insurance

Insuring your house, apartment,
or condominium and its contents

Liability insurance

Insuring your home office or small business

Insuring your cottage and recreational vehicles

What to do when you have a claim

Why Home Insurance?

WHETHER YOU'RE A STUDENT HEADING OFF TO UNIVERSITY, a young person renting your first apartment, a newlywed buying your first home, or an empty nester downsizing to a condominium, you need home insurance.

Home insurance is a "package" policy that generally covers not only your house itself (and any detached structures like garages and sheds), but also its contents, whether they're in the house or temporarily away from it. That means if your state-of-the-art skis are stolen while you're in the chalet warming up, they're covered, but only up to the dollar limit specified in your policy. Or perhaps a thief nabs your luggage during your Florida vacation. Again, your property insurance kicks in.

It also gives you legal protection if someone gets injured on your property and sues you, or if you accidentally injure someone or cause damage to a person's property. Let's say your neighbour trips on the loose board on your step, breaks her leg, and decides to sue you for damages. Or you go careening down a ski slope, accidentally slamming into a bystander and injuring him. In both cases, your liability insurance would come to your rescue, to cover not only any damages that you are ordered to pay, but also the legal fees to defend you in court. (See question 12, below.)

If you're planning to buy a home, you won't be able to borrow money for your mortgage unless the lending institution knows you have home insurance to cover the property in case of a big loss, like a fire.

Many young people moving into their first apartment—and even some veteran apartment dwellers—think they don't need home insurance. After all, they may not have much furniture, and they assume the landlord's insurance will cover any major damage to their unit. Wrong! If you cause the damage, you're legally responsible for it. If, for example, you drop a cigarette on the carpet and it starts a fire in the building, you would be liable for all the damage that you caused—not your landlord. Obviously, that could amount to a hefty chunk of money.

If you lost all your possessions in the fire, could you afford to replace them out of pocket? While you might not think you own much of value, it all adds up. Perhaps your CD collection alone would cost more to replace than you could afford. Your renters or tenants insurance would not only pay for the damage you caused *and* replace your belongings; it would also pay your additional living expenses if you had to live elsewhere while your unit was being repaired. It's a no-brainer.

Beware the exclusions!

Your home insurance won't protect you against every disaster that may come your way. Therefore, you need to know not only what your insurance covers but, more importantly, what it doesn't cover. These exceptions are called "exclusions," and there are plenty of them in any property policy. Here are some of them: your plumbing freezes and bursts while you are away on vacation and haven't arranged for anyone to check your house; a squirrel eats through your electrical wiring; your roof leaks and damages your ceiling; the nearby river overflows and floods your basement—the list goes on and on.

The important thing to remember is that your home insurance will protect your home against most *unforeseen* perils, but not against the inevitable. In other words, if you live in a flood plain, it's inevitable that your house will, at some point, be flooded; squirrels are notorious for getting into houses and wreaking havoc, so it is up to you to keep them out; and so on.

No insurance policy will protect against damage caused by wear and tear, rust, corrosion, or gradual deterioration. So if water seeps through your

CAUTION

Keep Your House in Shipshape Condition

It's up to you to properly maintain your house. Insurers will not cover damage from a leaking roof in need of repair, water that seeps in through the cracks in your foundation, a rusted-out oil tank that leaks, or any other damage related to wear and tear, gradual deterioration, or lack of maintenance.

leaky foundation, or your rusty oil tank leaks, don't bother calling your insurance agent or broker for help. (*Warning:* Water damage coverage is very tricky. Check page 45 for more details.)

Since brokers and agents do not always discuss these exclusions with policyholders, the onus is on consumers to ask the right questions (see checklist at the end of this chapter) or read their insurance policy—still a daunting task, despite the use by most insurers of so-called "plain language" in their policies.

Additional optional coverage, called an "endorsement," can be purchased to protect against some excluded perils but, in most cases, prevention is your only recourse. In fact, loss prevention is not only your best safeguard against loss or damage, insured or not, but it also keeps down insurance costs for all of us. After all, about 40 per cent of the cost of our home insurance goes to cover the cost of theft claims. Fewer claims, lower premiums. Your insurance company, or a national organization like the Insurance Bureau of Canada (see "Consumer Resources" in Appendix A) can provide you with plenty of tips on loss prevention.

All policies are not alike

When comparing cost and coverage, keep in mind that there are different kinds of homeowners policies; make sure you are comparing apples with apples when shopping for your home insurance. As a rule, you get what you pay for; the lower the premium, the less extensive the coverage. The insurance company with the cheapest price may not be the best choice come claims time either. For example, if one company is charging rates that are significantly lower than those of all the other insurers, chances are you will not get preferred service at claims time, when you really need it.

While most policies are fairly standard, there may be slight differences from one company to the next, for example, in the dollar limits that you can claim for specific items, or the exclusions. Unlike automobile insurance, home insurance rates are not regulated by the government, so prices and practices can vary, even for similar kinds of coverage. That's why it's a good idea to shop around. Try some independent brokers (who represent different insurance companies—ask them which ones they represent), direct writers (insurance companies who sell through their own agents), and direct-response insurers (who sell over the telephone). You may also get a better rate through a group insurer, such as an alumni or business association. (See chapter 1 for an explanation of the different ways in which insurance is sold.)

There are three kinds of homeowners policies: named-perils, broad-form, and comprehensive.

- *Named-perils*—also called "standard" or "basic." This is usually the cheapest kind of policy and offers the least protection, because it covers only those perils that are specifically listed, or named, in your policy. These commonly include fire, lightning, windstorm, explosion, riot, vandalism, and sometimes theft. While that might sound just fine, there are many perils that it doesn't cover. For example, if you lost your expensive leather jacket, it would not be covered under a named-perils policy even if that policy *did* cover theft, because it wasn't stolen from your house in a break-in.

- *Broad-form*—the intermediate level of coverage. This covers all perils for the building *except* those that are specifically listed as exclusions, but covers only "named perils" on the contents. Under a broad-form policy, the missing leather jacket may or may not be covered; when it comes to personal property, some broad-form policies cover only losses resulting from theft, not those items that simply go missing.

- *Comprehensive*—the most extensive, and expensive, coverage. A comprehensive policy covers everything that isn't specifically excluded, for both the house and the contents. Under this type of policy, the missing leather jacket would be covered, since this kind of loss is not excluded. However, even the comprehensive policy lists more than 30 exclusions, so don't be fooled by the term "all risk," which is often used by insurance providers to describe the broader form of coverage. It is anything but!

To make buying insurance easier and cheaper, some insurance companies are bundling property, automobile, and other kinds of coverages (like home office, cottage, or boat) into one "umbrella" package with a single payment and deductible. Of course, this arrangement is also more profitable for the broker or agent; instead of selling a series of smaller packages, the insurance provider can sell one larger one, and save on administrative costs. But if the package meets your needs and the savings are passed along to you, it's an option worth considering.

Your home insurance needs will change through different stages of your life. You might, for example, renovate your house, acquire some expensive jewellery, start a home business—there are many circumstances that could

Not Your Average Insurance Policies!

You can buy insurance to cover just about any kind of risk under the sun—and beyond. One enterprising British insurance broker even offered insurance against abduction by aliens! We don't know if there were any "takers."

Many of us have heard of forties movie star Betty Grable's insurance policy on her famous "million-dollar" legs by Lloyd's of London. While Lloyd's underwrites a wide variety of sizes and types of risks, including ships, buildings, fleets of cars, and air-planes, it is able to insure more unusual risks, like the following:

- *GRAINY PICTURE: A grain of rice with a portrait of the Queen and the Duke of Edinburgh engraved on it was insured at Lloyd's for the princely sum of $20,000.*

- *A MONSTER OF A RISK: Cutty Sark Whisky offered a one-million-pound prize to anyone who could capture the Loch Ness Monster alive. The company guarded against loss by taking out a Lloyd's policy. More recently, Cutty Sark offered a one-million-pound prize to the person producing an authentic extra-terrestrial device, again insuring against loss at Lloyd's.*

- *THE LAST LAUGH: A comedy-theatre group insured themselves against the risk of a member of their audience dying laughing.*

- *A MATTER OF TASTE: A food critic and gourmet insured his taste buds for 250,000 pounds, while a whisky distiller insured his nose.*

(Reprinted with permission of Lloyd's of London)

affect your insurance coverage. That's why you need to keep your agent or broker up to date. And don't wait for insurance providers to ask. They seldom do! You don't want to find out at claims time that you didn't have enough insurance to protect your assets.

Frequently Asked Questions... About Property Insurance

1. What does my homeowners policy generally cover?

Keeping in mind that there are three types of homeowners policies and that coverages do vary (see "All policies are not alike," page 20), the typical homeowners policy protects your house (including other structures on your property, like a tool shed) and personal property against loss or damage from a number of specified causes or "perils" (up to the limits outlined in the policy), including:

- Fire
- Lightning
- Wind and hail
- Theft
- Smoke (except that from fireplaces)
- Vandalism (as long as the premises are not vacant: see question 2)
- Explosion
- Accidental overflow of water (see question 29)
- Riot
- Aircraft
- Freezing of plumbing (some conditions apply: see question 29)
- Falling objects (except those caused by earthquake)
- Electrical current
- Vehicles (not including damage caused by a vehicle owned or operated by any of the insured policyholders)
- Breakage of glass

Most policies also cover your additional living expenses if you have to leave your house because of a major loss that's covered under your policy, for example, a fire (see question 33). It would also pay for the removal of debris, such as ash, dust, and destroyed building materials.

Your homeowners, renters, or condominium unit owners policy also covers your personal property, not only at your residence, but also at any other location. For example, if you drop your camera while trekking in Tibet, or your collection of CDs is stolen from your car, they're covered, as long as you can supply reasonable proof of ownership (see question 45).

Exception: Your home policy does not cover equipment that is used for business when it is away from your residence (see question 40).

Finally, your home policy gives you liability protection if you or someone you are responsible for injures another person or damages that individual's property, or if someone injures him- or herself on your property (see question 12).

Exception: Your home policy does not cover business-related liability; for example, a client who is injured at your residence while on business, or an injury or damage you cause while visiting a client (see question 41).

2. What does my homeowners policy not cover?

Again, it depends on the kind of homeowners policy, but generally, no policy will cover the following perils:

- Damage caused by wear and tear, rust, corrosion, or gradual deterioration, like a leaking roof or a rusty oil tank that springs a leak because it hasn't been properly maintained.
- Damage caused by vermin, rodents, and insects (see question 35).

SCENARIO

Moose On The Loose

Q. You live in the north country. One day, a rambunctious moose rams into your picture window and breaks it.
Are you covered?
A. That depends on what kind of homeowners policy you have. It wouldn't be covered under the most basic type of policy— named-perils—because it is not listed as one of the perils that the policy insures against. It may be covered if you have a broad-form (the intermediate-level) policy, and would certainly be covered if you have a comprehensive (the highest-level) homeowners policy.

- Damage caused by flood (see question 29) or earthquake (see question 38).
- Damage caused by water seepage, through the foundation or an open window, for example.

  Exceptions: water that leaks in from a public water main, or from your own swimming pool.
- Loss or damage to personal property on premises that have been vacant for more than 30 days (not just because you're on vacation, but because you have moved and do not intend to return).
- Water damage caused by pipes freezing if you are away more than four consecutive days, unless you have someone checking your house on a daily basis (see question 29).
- Damage caused by earth movement, including earthquakes (see question 38), landslide, and mud flow.
- Damage from volcanic eruption.
- Intentional loss by, or at the direction of, an insured; in other words, fraudulent claims.

You may be able to buy additional coverage, called an "endorsement," to protect you against a few of the perils that are normally excluded (see question 11), but no insurance will protect you against all of them. Be sure to ask your insurance provider what isn't covered under your policy. This list is not exhaustive!

In addition to items that are specifically excluded, there are some types of property that are not usually covered in a homeowners policy. These include: animals, birds, and fish; motor vehicles and accessories; boats and recreational vehicles; and property of boarders or renters, unless they are related to the insured. All of these can be insured under separate policies.

It might not seem fair that perils like earthquake, flood, or volcanic eruption are not covered under a homeowners policy. After all, what can you possibly do to prevent an earthquake? However, that is precisely the point. Insurance is intended to protect against the unpredictable and unforeseen. If you live in an earthquake zone, on a flood plain, or within range of a volcano, it is inevitable, at least in the eyes of insurers, that these disasters will strike at some point. That's a risk insurers aren't prepared to take. (It is possible to buy earthquake and flood insurance, but the cost is prohibitive for most consumers.)

3. How do I figure out how much coverage I need?

Your house should be insured for at least 80 per cent of the amount it would cost to rebuild it if it was totally destroyed, say, in a fire. That's called "replacement cost." It isn't the same as market value, because it doesn't include the value of the land (see question 9).

If your house is 2,000 square feet and it costs approximately $85 per square foot to rebuild in your area, the cost to replace your home would be approximately $170,000. Remember, if your house is destroyed, you can be paid only up to the amount of insurance stated in your policy, unless you have "guaranteed replacement cost." This coverage guarantees to make up any shortfall (often up to a specific limit) if you have underestimated the cost to rebuild your home. If you have this coverage—and many policies do include it—your house must be insured for 100 per cent, and not just 80 per cent, of the replacement cost. (Obviously, an insurance company will not be willing to pay to cover any shortfall in the cost of replacing your home if you haven't insured it for its full value in the first place.) Be sure to advise your insurer of any upgrades to your house, like marble flooring or special cabinets, that would be more expensive to replace, so must be taken into consideration in calculating your replacement cost.

Caution: Guaranteed replacement coverage will not pick up the additional cost of rebuilding a home to comply with updated building codes, unless you have purchased a special endorsement or it is provided for in your policy (see question 34).

TIP

Do You Have Enough?

Review your coverage on a regular basis—at least once a year at renewal time—so you can be sure you have adequate coverage. You may have acquired something new, renovated your house, started a business from your home—all these factors could have an impact on your insurance coverage.

In calculating your insurance needs, also be sure you have enough coverage to replace any valuables you may own, like furs, jewellery, and collectibles (see question 13), and enough liability protection to cover injuries to visitors on your property, or damage you may cause to someone else's property (see question 12).

4. How do insurance companies decide what to charge for home insurance?

They calculate the price according to a number of "risk factors"—the criteria by which insurance companies rate your property. Risk factors may include: construction materials (brick and stone houses are usually cheaper to insure than frame houses because of the greater risk of fire damage to frame houses); whether the owner lives in the house (owner-occupied houses are considered a better risk); and the location of the house (whether it's within 1,000 feet of a fire hydrant; rural homes more than five miles from a fire hall may be very expensive to insure, because the longer it takes firefighters to reach your house, the greater the potential for loss).

In pricing your policy, insurers will also consider the presence of any safety features, like burglar alarms, smoke detectors, and fire extinguishers. Most companies will offer a discount to homeowners who have installed this equipment.

Although they likely won't discuss it, insurers also take into account the "loss experience" for your particular area. If you live in an area that has been hit with many losses—more theft claims, more fires, more hail damage, or a combination of factors—you will probably pay more for your insurance than someone in a comparable house in a "safer" location.

In fact, an insurer might refuse to sell you home insurance if your house is not a good risk; for example, it's too old, not well enough maintained, or has an inadequate wiring or heating system. In that case, you would have to upgrade certain features in order to obtain insurance. Some insurance companies require an inspection on an older building before they agree to insure it, to verify that the plumbing, heating, and wiring meet current building codes. They might also refuse to insure an older home for its full replacement cost, unless it is in good condition.

The price of your insurance will also reflect the type of insurance policy you choose. The broader the coverage, the more you will pay for it.

5. How can I save money on my home insurance?

There are a number of ways you can save on your home insurance without skimping on coverage:

- Install safety devices, like burglar alarms, deadbolt locks, fire extinguishers, and smoke detectors. Most insurance companies offer a discount for these features, sometimes as much as 15 per cent (see question 4).
- Choose a high deductible (see question 10).
- Consider placing both your home and automobile insurance with the same insurance company (not to be confused with using the same broker for both). Many companies will offer a discount on your home insurance to entice you to do so (home insurance is generally more profitable for insurers than automobile insurance, so they like to offset potential automobile losses with the more lucrative home insurance). However, they are not allowed to make the insuring of one type of business (most likely, automobile) conditional on insuring the other (property). That is called "tied selling," and is not permitted.
- Try to keep your insurance record as claims-free as possible, and don't claim for small losses (see question 7), even if you weren't at fault. It may take only one claim for your premium to go up, so don't mar your record with a smaller claim that you can afford to pay out of pocket.
- Shop around, as insurance rates can vary considerably (see "All policies are not alike," page 20). However, keep the following points in mind:
  a. Compare apples with apples. There are different kinds of homeowners policies, so make sure you are comparing prices for the same kind of coverage (see "All policies are not alike," page 20).
  b. If you find a cheaper rate, don't switch insurance companies before your renewal date, or you will likely pay a penalty (see question 6).
  c. The company with the cheapest price may not be the best one to deal with at claims time. Also, you may need some optional coverage (see question 11) that is well worth the additional cost.
  d. Don't make a habit of switching from one insurance company to another at the drop of a few dollars. Many companies offer a discount

Doggone-It!

From our stable of strange but true insurance claims comes this gem which an Ontario insurance broker shared with *Canadian Insurance*, a national trade publication for the insurance industry.

"A Great Dane swallowed a pair of diamond stud earrings. The earrings, worth $1,500 to $2,000, were on the dresser in the bedroom, and the dog was in the room. Suddenly, the dog jumped up and swallowed them!

"I was laughing when I reported it to the insurer, but it was a legitimate claim; the policy was 'all-risk.' The woman's poor husband sifted through the dog's excrement for weeks, although the earrings were never found. The insurer paid the claim."

(Author's Note: *"All-risk" means the policy would pay for any perils that are not "excluded." This one was not excluded—nor excreted.*)

to policyholders who maintain a claims-free record for a specified period of time. And if you establish a long, and unblemished, relationship with one company, chances are it will treat you better when you *do* have a claim than would a new company that doesn't know you.

6. What happens if I find a better rate elsewhere and want to cancel my existing coverage?

You are free to cancel your coverage at any time, but your best bet is to wait until your policy comes up for renewal. Otherwise, you will likely have to pay a penalty for cancelling your coverage before the due date. This is called "short-rating," and insurers are legally entitled to do this to compensate for their administrative costs. The amount of the penalty will vary depending on how many months are left on your policy when you cancel it. The more months remaining, the higher the penalty. If, for example, your policy had been in force for just two months, you would be charged considerably more than one-sixth of the annual premium.

Often, consumers agree to be insured with one company, only to find they can get a better rate elsewhere. Because they may not have received the first policy yet in the mail, they assume it is a simple matter to cancel the coverage. Wrong! In fact, because the policy would have been in force for such a short period of time, you would be charged the highest penalty. It might even eat up all the money you thought you were saving by switching insurers.

As soon as you have agreed that a company will insure you—even if this agreement is only verbal and even if you haven't yet paid a cent—that commitment stands. Similarly, the insurer has made the same commitment to you. It is obligated to insure you from the time of that agreement, even if it hasn't yet received any money from you. So it works both ways.

If you decide to cancel come your renewal date, be sure to inform your insurer in writing. It's not enough to simply ignore your renewal notice. By sending you the renewal notice, the insurer has already made a commitment to you, so you, too, are on the hook for that coverage unless you tell the company otherwise before your renewal date.

CAUTION

You Cancel Prematurely, You Pay The Penalty

Have you found cheaper coverage elsewhere and want to cancel your existing policy? Don't be too hasty! While your insurance policy states that you can terminate your coverage at any time on request, you will likely be charged a penalty for cancelling before the renewal date. It could even end up costing you more than what you will save by switching insurers.

7. If I have several insurance claims, will I be penalized by the insurance company?

Probably, and almost certainly if you caused the loss or damage. Your premiums will rise considerably, and, if it was a very serious loss, or if you had several claims in which you were at fault, the insurance company might even choose not to renew your coverage when it comes due (see question 8).

If you didn't cause the loss, your insurance shouldn't be affected, but this is not always the case. For example, let's say your house was broken into twice in a one-year period. Then, a few months later, a tree falls on your roof. None of these claims are really your fault, but the insurer might conclude that you are a poor insurance risk and elect not to renew your coverage. In some cases, three strikes (in a short period of time) and you're out.

That's why it's not a good idea to claim for minor damage on your property policy, for example, a $400 stolen sweater or a broken window. Since you have to pay the deductible, it probably isn't worth it anyway (see question 10), and it just might come back to haunt you later. Save your claim for a major loss that you cannot afford to pay out of pocket. But why, you ask, should I pay for a loss myself when I buy insurance for that very reason? Good question! Don't think of your insurance as a cumulative payment that adds up over the years; think of it as buying protection for a one-year period against a large loss. If you ever experience a devastating loss, that is when insurance really pays its way.

8. Is the insurance company allowed to cancel my property coverage?

Yes, under certain conditions. But first, note that there is a difference between cancelling your policy part way through its term and simply choosing not to renew it when it comes due. If you have too many claims—at least by the insurance company's standards—it may decide not to renew your policy (see question 7).

Cancellation of your policy before its expiration date is another story. Although the insurer is not required to give any reason, it would likely cancel a policy for either of two reasons: the insured has not paid the premium; or has withheld important information from the insurer about the risk being insured.

If the insurer cancels your policy, it is legally required to give written notice, either delivered in person to your last known address, or sent by registered mail to the post office nearest you. If the notice is personally served, the cancellation takes effect five days after it has been delivered to you. If it is sent by registered mail, as most insurers choose to do, the cancellation becomes effective 15 days after the day it is delivered to your post office. If you don't pick it up from the post office, that's your problem—the cancellation takes effect anyway. The insurer must also refund your money on a pro rata basis for the amount of time remaining on your policy (as long as you paid your premium in the first place). In other words, if you paid for your policy for one year, and had six months remaining when your policy was cancelled, the insurer must refund you one half of your annual premium, unlike when an insured cancels a policy prematurely and usually must pay a penalty to the insurer (see question 6).

If your policy has been cancelled for non-payment, but you have a reasonable explanation for the mishap—maybe you thought your payment had been made but there was a mix-up—you can ask the insurer to resume your coverage. The insurer might be willing to do so if it believes you made an honest attempt to pay the premium.

Whatever the reason for it, a cancellation is not to be taken lightly; more than likely, the company that cancelled you will submit that information to a database used to track property claims history, so it will follow you to your next insurance company. If that company is willing to insure you, it will likely be at a higher rate. Your mortgage holder will also be informed, since your mortgage was conditional on you having insurance on your house. That won't exactly stand you in good stead.

9. If the market value of my house drops, will it cost less to insure it?

No. It is a common misconception among consumers that the cost of property insurance is related to the market value of their homes. Rather, the price of home insurance is related to how much it would cost to replace what you have lost at current prices (see question 3). Therefore, the insured value of your house must be updated regularly to keep pace with the increasing cost of replacement. Most insurers do this automatically for you.

Some consumers may think their insurer has overestimated the replacement cost of their house, and is consequently charging them too much to insure it. However, there are a couple of things to keep in mind. First of all, if your house were destroyed, the insurance would pay not only to rebuild it, but also to remove what was left of the original house.

Also, your homeowners insurance package covers much more than the cost to replace the building itself. It provides coverage for your personal property, the theft of items away from your home, liability, the cost of living away from home if your house was destroyed and had to be rebuilt, and so on.

Remember, too, that market value includes the land on which the house is built, which is not a factor in calculating your home insurance.

10. How high should my deductible be?

How much are you comfortable paying out of pocket? A deductible is the amount that you agree to pay, or have "deducted," from what the insurer pays, when you have a claim. You might want to opt for a high deductible, for a few reasons. First, you will save money on the cost of your insurance. The higher the deductible, the lower the premium. For example, a policy with a $250 deductible (you pay the first $250, the insurer pays the rest) could cost as much as 20 or 30 per cent more per year than one with a $500

TIP

Don't Sweat The Small Stuff!

If you have a small claim, you're probably better off to pay for the loss or damage yourself. Remember, you still have to pay the deductible and, depending on how high your deductible is, it may not be worthwhile to make a claim. Any claim, however small, goes on your insurance record. Too many claims in a short period of time can result in non-renewal of your policy, and could end up costing you a lot more in the long run to replace your insurance coverage.

or higher deductible. Therefore, if you choose a higher deductible, the additional amount that you would have to pay if you had a claim would likely be more than offset by the lower premium you would pay each year. Ask your insurance provider to show you the difference in premium between a higher deductible and a lower one.

Second, it is not in your best interest to make small claims anyway (see question 7), so why not remove the temptation by selecting a higher deductible? After all, you obviously wouldn't claim for a $500 stolen sweater if your deductible was $500, let alone $1,000. However, don't choose such a high deductible that you couldn't pay it out of pocket if you had a big claim tomorrow.

Note: You do not have to pay a deductible for liability claims or claims for "scheduled" items (see question 13).

11. What kinds of optional coverage can I buy?

The following are available to you:

- Sewer backup coverage, which is particularly useful if you live in a low-lying area (see question 29).
- Earthquake coverage (see question 38).
- Bylaw endorsement policy, to cover the additional cost of rebuilding your home to conform to stricter building codes (see question 34).
- Additional coverage for valuable items (see question 13) or home offices (see questions 40, 41). This may be done through an extension to your policy, or an "endorsement," which beefs up your coverage. An endorsement can increase the number of risks that you are insured against, cover property that would otherwise not be covered, or increase the amount the insurer will pay for a covered loss.

Also remember that you have a choice of homeowner policies: named perils, broad-form, or comprehensive (see "All policies are not alike," page 20).

12. Does my homeowners/tenants coverage protect me if someone injures themselves on my property?

Yes. Liability coverage is included with your homeowners or tenants package. This protects you not only against potential lawsuits from someone who injures themselves on your property, but also if you or any members of your household (including your pets) accidentally injure someone else, anywhere in the world.

For example, let's say you're skating on a canal in the Netherlands. You lose control and ram into another skater, knocking him down and cutting his face with your skate blade. If he sues you for damages, your insurance company will not only pay to defend you in court, but will also pay any awards made against you, up to a specified limit—generally anywhere from $100,000 to $1,000,000, depending on the policy.

Your insurance will also cover any reasonable medical expenses resulting from an accident that occurs on your property, or an unintentional injury that you cause to someone else. For example, if your Aunt Betty falls down your steep stairway and chips her front teeth, your insurance would likely cover the cost of her dental work, up to a specified limit. Or if your cocker spaniel bites your neighbour on the hand and she requires surgery (your neighbour, that is!), your insurance will pay for any related expenses, again up to a specified limit per person. Even worse, a teenager dives into your swimming pool, breaking his neck and becoming paralyzed for life. Again, your liability insurance will kick in.

Exceptions: injury or damage that is intentional; injuries that occur as a result of business—for example, clients who injure themselves when they visit you at your home office (see question 41); injuries or damage caused by the use, maintenance, or loading/unloading of motor vehicles, boats, or aircraft.

(see question 41)

TIP

Put Your Valuables On A "Schedule"

Even the broadest type of homeowners policy has limitations on what it pays for valuable items—like furs, jewellery, coin collections, silverware—that are stolen or damaged. Ask your insurance provider about "scheduling" these items—adding an endorsement that beefs up your coverage.

---

13. Are valuable items, like jewellery, insured under my home policy?

The total amount of coverage on your personal property varies from one company and policy to the next but it is usually about 70-80 per cent of the amount of coverage on your house. However, your policy places a limit on the amount you can claim for any one item (usually $2,000, in the case of jewellery). You would also have to pay the deductible. Therefore, you should "schedule" any valuable items, which means that each one will be named separately on your policy and insured for a specific amount. This is done by adding an "endorsement" or "floater" to your policy, an optional extra that beefs up your insurance coverage. Most insurance companies will ask you to get an appraisal on your jewellery if its value exceeds a certain amount (see question 14).

By scheduling an item, you not only cover it against theft, but also against loss. Let's say you accidentally flush your diamond ring down the toilet. A typical homeowners policy would insure your ring only against theft, not against a loss like that fateful flush. Of course, scheduling adds to the cost of your insurance, but it's a small price to pay if you lose an item that is worth much more than the limit allowed in your home policy. Another advantage is that scheduled items are not usually subject to a deductible.

You should also be aware that, when a piece of valuable jewellery is lost or stolen, you cannot receive a cash settlement for the amount that it has been insured. For example, if your stolen gold watch has been appraised and insured for $5,000, you cannot demand a $5,000 cash settlement, nor can you necessarily go out and spend $5,000 to replace it, thinking your insurance will pay that amount. The insurance company is obligated only to replace your watch with one of like kind and quality (see question 49). If the insurer can fulfill that obligation for less than $5,000, it has the right to do so. Be sure to keep any receipts, especially for items like cameras or camcorders that you would not have appraised, but for which you still need to verify ownership.

Also keep in mind that dollar limitations on your homeowners or tenants policy vary from one insurance company to another, not only in the amount, but also for the types of property specified under the different limits. For example, the limit could be as low as $300 for money and gold

This Diamond's Not Forever!

Q. You misplace your diamond engagement ring; you think it might have fallen down the heat register. Are you covered?

A. Only if you have a "comprehensive" policy, the broadest kind of homeowners policy available. The "named-perils," or "basic," policy does not cover loss of personal property, while the "broad-form" (intermediate-range) policy covers only losses caused by theft. The comprehensive policy, on the other hand, would cover a loss of this kind, but only up to the limit specified in the policy (probably $2,000). If that's not enough, you must add a special "endorsement" or "floater" to your policy to increase the coverage on your ring.

bullion, up to $10,000 for articles like tableware made of or plated with gold, silver, or pewter. (Also see question 40, on home office equipment.) Ask your insurance provider what the limits are for specific types of property under your particular homeowners or tenants policy.

Caution: If you keep your valuables in a safety deposit box, some insurance companies require you to inform them before removing the items, and advise them when the items will be returned. A charge may apply if you plan to keep the valuables out of the safety deposit box for longer than a specified time limit—often 10 days—and still want them to be insured.

14. How do I know how much insurance to buy on my jewellery?

You should have your jewellery appraised by an independent appraisal firm that is not connected with buying and selling jewellery. Ideally, the firm should be accredited, meaning that it has met the criteria established by the Canadian Jeweller's Institute for performing appraisals. The appraisal should be updated on a regular basis—usually every three to seven years—as values can fluctuate.

Don't confuse a sales receipt with an appraisal; a sales receipt proves only how much you paid for the item, not its actual value. An appraisal, on the other hand, will provide you, not only with proof of value, but with a detailed description of the item. That way, if an item is lost, damaged, or stolen, your insurer can replace it with one that is as similar as possible in style and quality to the original. Although you likely have to pay for the appraisal yourself, it's a worthwhile investment, as it will help you insure your jewellery for its true value. Otherwise, you might not buy enough insurance to replace your valuables or, conversely, you might buy more than you need.

15. I live in an apartment. Do I still need home insurance?

Absolutely! There are several reasons why apartment dwellers and other renters need tenants insurance. First, think of all the personal property that you own—CDs, furniture, stereo equipment, clothing, dishes, and so on. Could you replace all those items in one fell swoop if they were lost in, say, a fire? The landlord has insurance on the building itself, but not on your personal possessions. A tenants package policy would not only replace your personal belongings (to any limits specified in the policy), but would also pay

SCENARIO

Saving Your Bacon

Q. You leave some bacon cooking on the stove in your apartment while you go to answer the phone. A grease fire starts, causing considerable smoke damage to your kitchen. Are you covered?

A. Only if you have tenants insurance. You, not your landlord, are responsible for the damage, since you caused it. If you have a tenants package policy, however, the liability portion will cover the damage. It will also cover your additional living expenses if the damage is so extensive that you have to move out while repairs are being made to the premises.

additional living expenses if you needed to live elsewhere while your apartment was being repaired (see question 33). It would also come to your rescue if your brand-new digital camera, for example, was stolen from your car, or perhaps from your hotel room in Rome, not just from your apartment.

And that's not all. Tenants insurance also provides you with liability coverage. Let's say you leave the stove on in your apartment. It causes a fire that spreads throughout the building. You would be liable for that damage, since you caused it. Imagine how much *that* could cost you if you didn't have insurance! A tenants policy would protect you against this calamity.

Generally tenants insurance is relatively inexpensive, because, unlike a homeowners policy, it does not insure the building, only the contents of your unit. (*Note:* Condominium owners need special coverage—see question 23.)

16. I am going away to college this year and will be renting an apartment. Do I need separate insurance, or am I covered under my parents' homeowners policy?

Most homeowners, tenants, and condominium unit owners policies cover the personal property of all members of the family who live in the insured residence while they are *temporarily* away. (Some insurance policies even refer specifically to students who are temporarily living away from home to attend college or university.) However, there may be a limit on the coverage, possibly as low as $2,500 on property used by students while away at college.

That may not be enough to cover valuable items that you might be taking with you—a laptop computer, for example. In that case, you would need to arrange for additional coverage for these items before you leave.

Caution: The policy does not cover anything that you buy for your apartment that you will not be taking back home with you—furniture, for example. That's because it isn't considered property that is temporarily away from your permanent residence; the furniture wasn't there when you left for college, so it won't be there when you return.

The bottom line: don't head off for the hallowed halls of higher education without learning first about your insurance. Verify with your insurance provider that you are covered under your parents' policy, and for what amount. And ask about any restrictions.

17. I live with two roommates. Do we need separate home insurance policies?

Check with your insurance provider, but usually it is best if all of you are covered under the same policy. However, it is also possible for each of you to purchase a separate policy. Remember, if only one of you purchases the policy in his or her own name, the other two will not be covered.

18. What kind of insurance do I need for my cottage?

You can insure your cottage either separately or with your homeowners or tenants policy. Since you already have personal liability coverage with your home policy (check with your insurance provider to make sure it is extended to your cottage as well), you need insurance only on the building itself and the contents of your cottage. This is called a "dwelling" policy.

Coverage on a cottage is usually subject to limits. Insurers are not willing to go out on a limb to insure your rustic lakeside retreat because of the greater risk involved in doing so. A cottage is not occupied year-round, nor is it usually close to firefighting services and water mains, so it is more prone to burglary and fire and water damage than your permanent residence.

Insurance against burglary and vandalism is optional. Burglary coverage will kick in only if your property shows signs of forced entry. This differs from your homeowners policy, which usually covers theft even in the absence of forced entry. Your cottage would also not be covered if the roof collapsed due to an accumulation of snow, whereas your home most likely would be. Ask your insurance provider what *isn't* covered on your cottage policy, and what limits exist on the coverage that you do have.

19. My mother-in-law lives with us. Does she need separate insurance?

As a member of your family, she should be covered under your homeowners or tenants policy, but check with your insurance provider to find out the extent of her coverage.

20. If I rent out my basement, are my tenants covered under my homeowners policy?

No. Your homeowners policy covers the building (including the basement), your personal property, and your personal liability. However, your tenants' personal belongings and their liability are not covered by your policy. They need to buy a tenants package policy (see question 15). You should notify your insurance company if you rent out your basement, because that changes the risk for the insurer.

21. I have a second home that I rent out. What kind of insurance do I need for that?

First, you need a separate "dwelling" policy to insure the building. (See question 18.) You don't need to insure the contents unless you are renting it furnished or you have personal belongings there (your tenants need to buy their own insurance to cover their personal belongings and liability). You also need to add an endorsement, or extension, to your homeowners policy to cover the additional liability risk. (See question 13.) After all, you have *two* properties where someone could injure themselves and hold you responsible. Your insurance policy needs to reflect that greater risk.

22. Are my belongings covered while I am moving from one residence to another?

It depends. Many home policies do cover items against loss or damage while in transit. However, if you hire a moving company, your belongings may not be insured against breakage while they are in the mover's care. Therefore, you should ask the moving company about the insurance it offers, and ask your insurance provider about covering items that may be at both your old and new locations on moving day.

23. I am moving to a condominium. What kind of insurance do I need?

You need special insurance designed for condominium unit owners. Condominium insurance differs from homeowners or tenants insurance in a number of ways. The building and your unit are covered by a "master policy"

Condo Owners Need Special Coverage

Don't substitute tenants insurance for condominium unit owner's insurance. If you own a condominium, you need special coverage for your unit beyond what a tenants package policy provides. Exception: If your condo corporation is not registered, you may need tenants insurance in the interim. As soon as the corporation is registered, you can convert your insurance to a condo policy.

provided by the condominium corporation, which is paid as part of your monthly condominium fees. That protects not only the "common" elements of the condominium—elevators, parking garages, landscaping, etc.—but usually the units themselves as well, including any standard fixtures, like kitchen counters and cabinets, floor coverings, and bathroom vanities.

However, you still need a separate policy, called condominium unit owners insurance. This covers your personal property, personal liability, and any upgrades that you may have made to your unit; for example, if you installed hardwood flooring, added new wallcoverings, or remodeled your kitchen. If you aren't the original owner of the unit, make sure you are aware of any upgrades so you can insure them adequately.

Choose an insurance provider who specializes in condominium unit owners insurance to ensure there are no gaps in coverage between the condominium master policy and your individual unit owner's policy. And don't make the mistake of buying a tenants insurance package instead, unless your condominium development has not been incorporated (see "Caution," below). Condominium unit owner policies have extra features that tenants insurance does not, such as protection against losses that aren't covered under the condominium master policy.

You will have to pay a deductible on both the master policy and the condominium unit owners policy if you have a claim in which both policies apply.

Caution: Your condominium development must be incorporated before you can buy a separate condominium insurance policy. That means that the condominium owners must sell a certain percentage of condos before they can apply to have the corporation registered. If your condominium development is not registered, you have to be insured under a renter's policy; it can be converted to a condominium policy once registration has taken place. Also be aware that every condominium development has unique features that could change the way in which the master policy operates. Make sure you know which policy covers what, and when.

24. Are other buildings on my property covered, like my backyard shed?

Yes. Sheds, detached garages, and other outdoor structures are covered under your homeowners policy, usually up to a limit of 10 per cent of your total coverage.

Exception: Barns and any outbuildings that are used for business or rented to others.

Your homeowners policy also covers your plants and shrubs (up to 5 per cent of your total coverage), but not your lawn (see question 39).

25. How do I insure my recreational vehicles, like boats and Jet Skis?

Most insurance companies provide limited coverage under your homeowners or tenants policy for damage to small boats, like canoes, small powerboats, and sailboats. For larger boats, however, you need to purchase separate insurance. The cost will vary according to the size, type, and value of the boat, and where you use it. Other personal watercraft, like Jet Skis,

STRANGE BUT TRUE

That Danged New Math

A man in Boston claimed to his insurer that his 25-foot power-boat had been stolen from a locked garage. Upon investigation, reported the Insurance Fraud Bureau of Massachusetts, it was determined that the garage measured just 19 feet long. Oops!

may also be covered under your homeowners or tenants policy to a limited extent, but check with your insurance provider—you may need additional coverage.

You also need liability coverage for your recreational vehicle, in case it injures someone or damages someone else's property. Your homeowners insurance usually provides liability coverage for ownership of trailers (except when attached to a motor vehicle), small boats, golf carts on a golf course, self-propelled lawn mowers, snow blowers, garden tractors, and motorized wheelchairs. However, you will need separate liability coverage for larger watercraft.

All-terrain vehicles and snowmobiles also require separate insurance.

26. I am a snowbird who goes south for the winter. Do I have to inform my insurer?

No. You are under no obligation to inform your insurer before migrating to sunnier climes. However, you *are* obligated either to shut off your water and drain the pipes and fixtures, or have a competent person check your house daily to ensure the heat is on and that your pipes do not freeze and burst if there is a power failure. This requirement applies to anyone who leaves their home unoccupied for more than four consecutive days. Unless you have made the above arrangements, your insurance will not cover you in the event of water damage from burst pipes. If, on the other hand, your pipes were to freeze and burst despite being checked daily, the damage would likely be covered.

CAUTION

Winter Water Warning

If you go away for more than four consecutive days during the winter season, make sure you either turn off your water and drain the pipes, or have a competent person check your house every day. Otherwise, there's no coverage if your pipes freeze and burst.

Of course, no matter how long you plan to be away, you should make sure your house has a lived-in look: install variable timers on the light switches, and arrange to have someone shovel your driveway/walkway and clear flyers from the porch.

27. If something is stolen from my car, am I covered?

Yes. Your homeowners or tenants policy covers any items stolen from your car that are not part of the car. (Items that *are* part of your car, like its stereo system, would be insured under the comprehensive coverage on your automobile policy instead.) You will have to pay the deductible, however, so it wouldn't make sense to claim for a $500 sweater that was stolen from your car if your deductible is $500—or even if it's $250 (see question 7). You will also need to verify the ownership of any articles that you claim, likely through receipts.

Of course, only those items that are normally covered under your homeowners or tenants policy will be insured if they are stolen from your car. A laptop computer that is used for business, for example, would not be covered unless you had a separate business policy (see question 40).

28. If I take something with me on vacation and it is stolen, am I covered?

Don't worry—your property insurance covers anything temporarily removed from your home, whether it be in Timmins or Timbuktu. You have to pay the deductible, however, and there are limits on the amount you can claim (see question 13). If the limit specified in your policy is not high enough for your needs, you should buy an endorsement, or "floater," to boost your coverage.

Caution: Even if you have a legitimate claim, don't fall into the trap of making too many small claims (see questions 7 and 27).

29. Does my insurance cover a flood in the basement?

Probably not. Your homeowners policy generally covers accidental discharge or overflow of water, but not floodwater or water seepage that is repeated or continuous, through a cracked basement wall, for example. Therefore, if you go downstairs one day to find your basement swimming in water, your insurance will cover the damage only if the water came up through the main drain *and* you have sewer backup coverage, which is an optional endorsement (see question 11). Most homeowners policies do provide this option, but you may have to ask for it. There may also be a dollar limit on this coverage, especially in flood-prone areas.

If your basement was flooded as a result of a river overflowing, you would not be covered. The insurance industry does not insure against flooding, because, the thinking goes, if you live in an area that can be flooded, sooner or later, it will be. Insurance is intended to protect against the sudden and accidental, not the inevitable. Although flood insurance does exist, it is generally too expensive for the average homeowner and is not always available in flood-prone areas. If your house is near a river, keep your pipes intact and free of debris, add weeping tiles where needed, and possibly install a new sump pump.

Water seepage, perhaps through a leaky foundation or as a result of blocked drains from falling leaves, is not covered because this kind of problem is caused by a lack of maintenance, and is therefore preventable. The same thing goes for a leaky roof.

If, on the other hand, you left your tub faucet running while you went to answer the phone and your bathtub overflowed, that damage would be covered, since it is considered "sudden and accidental." Similarly, if a windstorm created a hole in your house and water leaked through, you'd be covered. On the other hand, if you left your window open and water

---

CAUTION

Water, Water Everywhere—But Are You Covered?

If you live near a flood plain, see about buying sewer backup coverage, sold as an optional endorsement to your homeowners policy. However, no insurance policy will protect against water damage as a result of a river overflowing.

came in, you may or may not be covered, depending on the type of policy you have (see "All policies are not alike," page 20).

Water damage could also result from frozen pipes that burst. In this case, you would be covered if the house was occupied at the time of the accident. However, if you were away more than four consecutive days when it happened, you would not be covered, unless you had a competent person checking your house every day. If that is not the case, play it safe by shutting off the water supply and draining the pipes before you leave.

Obviously, water damage is a very complicated issue. Coverage may vary from one policy to the next; check with your insurance provider to see which perils are covered and, just as important, which ones are not, so you don't end up in hot water at claims time.

30. My roof was damaged in a hailstorm. Will my insurance pay to replace it?

If only part of the roof was damaged, your insurance will pay to replace only the damaged portion. You can't expect the insurer to replace the entire roof, unless you are prepared to pay the difference in cost yourself. Otherwise, you'd be profiting from your misfortune. Insurance is intended only to put things back to the way they were before the damage, not replace them with something better.

In the case of an older roof whose useful life span is just about up, you will be paid a depreciated amount, which could be only about 25 per cent of the cost of a new roof.

31. What happens if the company insuring my property goes out of business?

No problem. The Property and Casualty Insurance Compensation Corporation (PACICC) will step in. PACICC is an organization funded by the property and casualty insurers—those companies that sell insurance for your homes, cars, and other property in Canada—to protect against insolvencies. In the unlikely event that your insurer does go out of business, contact your agent or broker as soon as possible to have your policies replaced. This must be done within 45 days of the date of the court order declaring the company bankrupt. (See chapter 1 for more details about insurer insolvencies.)

32. If there is a power failure, and everything in my freezer is damaged, does my insurance cover it?

Yes. You would be covered up to a maximum of $2,000, with no deductible. The insurance would cover not only the spoiled food, but also any damage to the freezer liner from the spoiled food, as well as any expenses incurred in storing food while the freezer was being repaired.

Caution: You are not covered if someone simply pulls the plug, accidentally or not, on your freezer, like your rambunctious Gretzky wannabe as he practises his stickhandling. That's because pulling the plug is considered preventable on your part, whereas a mechanical breakdown or a general power failure is unavoidable, and therefore, insurable.

33. What does my insurance cover if my house is destroyed in a fire?

Your insurance will cover the contents of your house to the amount specified in your policy, as well as the cost to repair or rebuild your home (assuming you have replacement cost, as most policies do) for the value it is insured in your policy.

Furthermore, your insurance will pay for any additional living expenses you incur while waiting for your house to be repaired, usually up to a maximum of 20 per cent of the total insurance on your house. These costs could include relocation and storage expenses, food and lodging if you have to stay in a hotel, additional transportation costs to and from school or work, or maybe furniture rental for a temporary residence. Of course, your insurer won't foot the bill for you to live in a five-star hotel, but will keep you in the style to which you were accustomed, within reason. Be sure to save all related receipts. The insurer will usually advance a cheque to cover these costs before your final claim settlement is made. For this coverage to kick in, the peril that destroyed your house must be one that your policy insures against (fire is an insured peril; flood and earthquake are not), and the damage must make your house unfit to live in while it is being repaired. Apartment and condominium dwellers have the same coverage with their property policies, but the total sum available is calculated on the amount of insurance on the contents, rather than on the building.

34. If I have to rebuild my house or cottage to conform to stricter building codes, does my insurance cover it?

No. It will cover this additional expense only if you have purchased an optional "bylaw" endorsement on your policy. While some policies do offer this coverage, you may have to purchase it separately.

35. Does my homeowners policy cover damage caused by animals like squirrels and raccoons?

No. Damage caused by "vermin"—insects, bugs (including termites!), and small animals like squirrels, skunks, mice, rats, woodchucks, birds, and raccoons—is "excluded" from your policy, meaning it is not covered. That is because these animals are known for their destructive behaviour, and therefore, insurance companies insist it is the homeowner's responsibility to keep them from getting into the house in the first place.

If, on the other hand, your dog goes on a rampage and wrecks your sofa, the damage would likely be covered. The reasoning is that dogs are not normally destructive, and therefore, the damage could not have been predicted.

CAUTION

Out Varmints!

Take every precaution to prevent rodents, insects, raccoons, and other vermin from getting into your house. No insurance policy will cover damage caused by these varmints.

36. Do I have to tell my insurer if I renovate my house?

Yes. If you have guaranteed replacement cost (see question 3) on your policy, you must inform your insurer of any renovations immediately. Guaranteed replacement cost means that, if your house was destroyed, and it cost more than the value of the policy to rebuild it, this coverage would make up the shortfall, subject to certain limits. Therefore, the insurer must be aware of any changes so it can insure your house for its full replacement value.

Even if you don't have guaranteed replacement cost, it is in your own interest to inform your insurer of any renovations. Otherwise, you could end up underinsured. After all, it will cost more to replace your remodeled house than it would the original, so you may need additional coverage. If you don't tell your insurance company about the renovation, your oversight could prevent you from claiming the full replacement value if your house is destroyed.

On the brighter side, your renovation may save you money on your insurance premium if, for example, you replaced old plumbing and wiring with new.

Caution: Don't wait until the renovation is complete before you increase your coverage. If your addition is damaged or destroyed before you have it insured, you could be on the hook for the cost of repairing or rebuilding it.

37. If someone succumbs to carbon monoxide poisoning in my house, would that be covered under my homeowners policy?

It depends on who the victim was. Your homeowners liability coverage does not apply to injuries sustained by you or members of your immediate household. However, if the unfortunate victim was someone other than those who are insured under your policy, your liability coverage would come into play, just as it would if someone tripped on your loose floorboard or fell into your empty swimming pool.

38. Am I covered if my house gets hit by a tornado or earthquake?

Tornado, yes; earthquake, no. Tornadoes are covered under the "wind or hailstorm" peril, but earthquakes require separate insurance, and it doesn't come cheap.

Your current homeowners policy will likely cover any damage not caused *directly* by the earthquake; for example, a fire caused by escaping gas from a line that has been ruptured by the quake. However, some insurers exclude "fire following" an earthquake from homeowners policies, so check with your insurance provider to see if there are any special terms relating to this peril.

Even if your homeowners policy will cover fire following an earthquake, it most definitely will not cover damage caused by the actual shaking movement of the earth. For that, you need separate earthquake insurance. Not only is that coverage very expensive, but it usually carries a high deductible. However, if you live anywhere near a fault line—British Columbia, the Ottawa Valley, parts of Quebec—it might be well worth the investment. Don't expect your homeowners policy to pick up the pieces.

39. Does my insurance cover damage to my lawn and shrubs caused by someone else's car?

As far as the lawn goes, you're out of luck. Lawns are not normally insured because they are so easily damaged. Trees, plants, and shrubs, on the other hand, are insured under your homeowners policy, but there's usually a limit of $500 for any one plant, and a maximum limit of 5 per cent of the total insurance on your house.

This coverage also includes the cost of removing any debris from your property if your uprooted plants need to be hauled away. Since you have to

---

SCENARIO

Does Not Compute

Q. You are walking across the parking lot to your client's office, when you drop your laptop computer. It lands with a sickening thud on the pavement, shattered beyond repair. Is it covered?
A. Only if you have a business policy. Your laptop is covered while it's safe at home (at least up to a specific limit), but once it goes on the road with you, it needs special coverage if it's used for business.

pay the deductible, however, it may not always be feasible to claim for damaged trees, plants, and shrubs. For example, if your tree is damaged, but your deductible is $500, you wouldn't receive a cent. That's because the most you could recover for your tree is $500, which is exactly what you would have to pay for your deductible. In that case, if you know who caused the damage, your only recourse is to ask that person to pay for the tree.

40. I have a home office. Do I need special insurance on my office equipment?

Probably. Your homeowners insurance will cover personal property used for business purposes, but only up to a certain limit—usually $2,000 in all. That wouldn't go far if someone broke into your house and stole, say, your laptop, fax machine, and printer. Therefore, if you have invested a lot of money in equipment for your home business, whether it be computers or woodworking tools, consider buying a business package policy. Doing this will not only cover your equipment, it will also protect you against any liability associated with your business, another peril that is not covered under your homeowners policy (see question 41).

You should also have a separate business policy (or a business extension on your existing homeowners/tenants policy) if any of your equipment travels with you, because business equipment is covered under your homeowners policy only while it is in your home, and then only to the limit specified. Therefore, if you are in the habit of bringing your state-of-the-art laptop to client meetings, for example, make sure it is adequately protected.

Whatever your home business, discuss it with your insurance provider. The coverage you need may vary depending on the nature of your business.

41. Do I need special liability insurance for my home office?

Yes. Say a client comes to visit you in your home. She trips and falls down the stairs to your basement office, injuring herself, and decides to sue you. Your homeowners/tenants policy won't protect you. In this kind of situation, you need a special home business package policy. This would not only cover any damages awarded against you, but would also pay to defend you in the lawsuit.

Your home business liability coverage will also protect you if you accidentally damage a client's property. For example, the client you are visiting asks you to move some paint cans that are sitting in her soon-to-be-painted office. You are only too eager to help (after all, she's a client!), but alas, as you lift the first can, it slips from your grasp and falls on the floor, oozing paint all over her expensive carpeting. Your client rewards you for your efforts by suing you. Again, your home business policy would come to your rescue, whereas your homeowners insurance would not. If the same incident had occurred while you were on a social, rather than a business, visit, it would be a different story; in that case, your homeowners insurance *would* cover you.

If you are a consultant, or someone who is paid to give advice, you may also need "errors and omissions" insurance. This covers you in the event that the advice you give to your client is inaccurate or incomplete, and that person's business suffers as a result. This kind of insurance is often available more economically through professional associations.

And if you supply a product, or install or service something, you may also need an extension to your business policy called "completed operations coverage." This covers you if injury or damage occurs as a result of your work *after* you have finished your job and left your client's premises.

SCENARIO

The Case of the Clumsy Client

Q. Your client comes to visit you at your home office. On the way in the front door, he slips on your floor mat, falls, and breaks his ankle. He sues you for damages. Are you covered?

A. Only if you have a special home business package policy that includes liability coverage. If the accident had not been business-related, your homeowners or tenants liability insurance would protect you. However, because this case involved a client, you need special coverage.

42. I have a small business. What kind of coverage do I need?

Depending on the type of business you are in, you may need some or all of the following:

- business-interruption insurance, which compensates for the income lost if your business is unable to operate for a period of time due to disaster-related damage;
- liability insurance, in case someone suffers an injury or damage because of something your business did or did not do;
- errors and omissions coverage, if you are in the position of offering advice to clients (see question 41);
- possibly life, health, and disability insurance, for both yourself and your employees;
- workers' compensation, should an employee become injured as a result of a job-related accident or suffer an illness attributable to a workplace cause;
- and possibly a commercial automobile policy if you need protection for your business against damage caused to other people or property by your vehicle, as well as protection against damage to your own vehicle. A commercial automobile policy may also cover your employees when they are operating their personal cars for your business.

This list is by no means exhaustive. Find an insurance provider that specializes in commercial insurance who can insure your business against the most critical potential losses, as well as suggest some loss-prevention measures to keep disaster from striking.

The Claims Scenario

43. How do I make a claim if something is damaged or stolen?

In the case of a theft, notify the police immediately, and in all cases, inform your insurance provider (whether it be an agent, broker, or the company itself) as soon as possible. Many companies and brokers today offer a 24-hour hotline for reporting claims. If immediate temporary repairs are required—say, your patio door was pried open in a break-in—your insurer may help arrange assistance.

If a theft has occurred, be prepared to supply reasonable evidence to support your claim: for example, receipts, photographs, video inventory.

Your insurance provider will likely appoint an adjuster to settle your claim. This person may be an employee of the insurance company or an "independent" adjuster contracted by the insurance company. The adjuster will investigate your claim, and make a recommendation to the insurance company whether to pay the full amount you requested, pay part of what you requested, or refuse the claim and make no payment. The final decision rests with the insurance company, who will notify you. If you think the amount offered is too low, you do not have to accept it (see question 46), but the onus is on you to prove why a higher payment is justified.

Remember, you also have to pay a deductible (your portion of the claim), except in the case of a "scheduled" item (see question 13).

44. When should I NOT make a claim?

It may be best not to make a claim under the following circumstances:

- If it is for only a small amount of money, particularly if your deductible is high. For example, if your deductible is $500, and you suffer a loss in the amount of, say, $800, it probably isn't worthwhile to make a claim for only $300. From the consumer's point of view, however, it makes perfect sense. After all, $300 *is* a significant amount of money, and you've been faithfully paying your insurance all these years. But that small claim could come back to haunt you. It will go on your record, and should you have another claim within a short period of time, you could end up paying more in the long run, in the form of increased premiums, than if you had not reported the smaller claim.
- If you have more than one recent claim. Unless you have suffered a very large loss that you cannot afford to pay yourself, it's best not to claim in this case. Too many claims—for example, three theft claims in as many years—could result in a large increase in premium, or even non-renewal of your insurance (see question 7).

45. What information or proof do I need to make a claim?

The more you have, the easier it is to settle your claim. Insurance companies, concerned about the high cost of insurance fraud, are vigilant when it comes to settling claims. In the case of a complete loss, like a fire, it helps if you already have an inventory of your home, whether it be a list of all your possessions or, ideally, a video in which you verbally list the items and their date and cost of purchase. Include serial numbers as well, when applicable. You could use professional video-inventory services, but you would have to pay for that yourself. Photographs and a tape recorder can also be useful. Be sure to store any lists, photographs, audiocassettes, or videotapes off-premises.

Also save receipts for expensive items. Receipts may be required to have your claim resolved. While the majority of consumers are honest, insurance companies will not replace expensive items with no proof of ownership.

46. What do I do if I disagree with my claim settlement?

First, make sure you read, and understand, your policy. Many disagreements arise because policyholders do not understand the conditions of their coverage, especially the exclusions (what is *not* covered). Many insurance providers do not adequately explain the policy to the customer at the time of purchase (or renewal). But consumers must also shoulder some of the responsibility for ensuring they understand what they are buying (and *not* buying!).

If, however, you have checked your policy and still disagree with your claim settlement, ask to speak with the claims manager at the insurance company and explain your situation. If that brings no results, contact the ombudsperson at the insurance company, if there is one (in Ontario, it is a requirement under the current insurance regulations). Next, contact the organization responsible for regulating insurance matters in your province (see "Consumer Resources" in Appendix A for more information), but be prepared to submit your claim in writing with supporting documentation.

You might also contact the Consumer Information Centre at the Insurance Bureau of Canada (see Appendix A), and seek the advice of one of the information officers.

If all else fails, you may choose to consult a lawyer who specializes in insurance litigation. If you retain a lawyer, make sure you understand the attorney's fee structure. Is it an hourly rate or is it a lump sum payable on settlement? (The latter is more common in cases involving bodily injury.) Another alternative is to use the services of a public adjuster, who is retained by the consumer rather than the insurance company, and is paid

Inquiring Minds Want Proof!

This claim, as reported to *Canadian Insurance* magazine by a
Regina-based broker, didn't hold water with the insurer.

"One unusual claim we had concerned a powerboat that had just
been in the shop, at the insurance company's expense.
No sooner had the boat been repaired when it became the subject
of another claim.

"Just after the owner picked up the boat, his son took it out on
the road, on a trailer hitched to the back of the car. He had to
stop suddenly and the boat somehow lifted off the trailer and
landed on top of the car, damaging both. Of course, the
insurance company refused to believe the story of how it
happened. But somehow, The National Enquirer *in the*
United States got wind of it, and ran a story with a full-color
photo. Only then was the claim accepted and paid for."

by the consumer on a contingency basis. Public adjusters are not common
in Canada, but they do exist; check the Yellow Pages.

If the problem lies with the broker or agent not having sold you the prop-
er coverage in the first place, you may have to seek restitution through the
courts. All agents and brokers carry "errors and omissions" insurance to
protect themselves against that possibility.

47. If a friend breaks something in my house, can I claim for it under my homeowners policy?

No. If you didn't break it, you shouldn't claim for it. The person who caused
the damage must take the rap. In that case, your insurer will settle your
claim, as long as the damaged item was insured under your homeowners or
tenants policy, and will then try to recover the money it paid you from the
person who was responsible for the damage. This is called "subrogation."

It's as if you were to sue the responsible party yourself for damages, except that you get the money faster from your insurer.

Caution: Don't tell the person who caused the damage that you will claim for it under your homeowners or tenants policy; this approach might backfire. For example, your friend Suzy breaks your antique vase. You tell her not to worry about it, that it is covered under your homeowners policy. The insurance company pays your claim, and then goes after Suzy for the money that it has already paid you. But Suzy says you told her she wouldn't have to pay, that you would claim for the damage yourself. That means you have denied your insurer the chance to recover its money from Suzy. Consequently, your insurer might not pay you the full amount for your claim, and all because you tried to let Suzy off the hook.

48. What do I do if I know someone has made a false claim?

It is a crime to exaggerate an insurance claim or file a false one. Report it to Crime Stoppers, at 1-800-222-TIPS. All calls are anonymous, and you could receive a reward based on the value of funds recovered or fraudulent claims denied. Insurance fraud costs the industry an estimated $1.3 billion a year. Although many consumers might dismiss insurance fraud as the insurance companies' problem, it is actually the policyholders who pay the price for it, through increased premiums. Therefore, it's in your best interest to report cheaters.

49. What if I decide not to replace an item that has been damaged or stolen, or if I want to replace it with something different? Can I get the cash for it instead?

Yes, but you will receive only "actual cash value" for it. That's the cost to replace the item *less* depreciation. Depreciation takes into account the estimated wear and tear on the item that was damaged, or the loss in value because of aging and use.

Most homeowners policies sold today pay "replacement cost" on lost or damaged property. That means that you must use the insurance money to replace what you lost with something that is as similar as possible to the lost/damaged item in functionality and quality. Your insurer may request a sales receipt as proof that you have done so. The advantage of replacement

Fraud Hall Of Shamers

While insurance fraud is no laughing matter, you have to chuckle at the sheer stupidity of these would-be fraud artists, elected by the Canadian Coalition Against Insurance Fraud to its Fraud Hall of Shame.

- A BAD CASE OF FREEZER BURN: *Following an electrical failure in his neighbourhood, a man submitted a claim for spoiled food. Nothing wrong with that. However, he also claimed that his leather jacket, which he said he stored in the freezer "to protect the leather," had been ruined as well. Not surprisingly, this claim was put on ice.*

- CRIME RING: *On a claim for a break-and-enter, one man noted that his $7,000 diamond ring had been stolen. He said he had bought it from a friend, but his story lacked a ring of truth to the insurance company. Upon investigation, it found that the friend had been arrested a short time earlier on narcotics charges. The diamond ring did, in fact, exist, but it had been seized by police and was in an RCMP evidence room at the time the supposed break-and-enter occurred.*

- TIMING IS EVERYTHING: *To finance a shopping spree, a man decided to stage a break-in of his own car. He had the perfect alibi for the insurance company in case suspicion was cast his way—he was shopping when the break-in occurred. Just one hitch. The adjuster checked the man's cell phone records and shopping receipts. How could he have been shopping at the time of the break-in, when he made his 911 call before he went into the store? Add attempted insurance fraud to his credit woes.*

cost is that it doesn't take depreciation into account when paying a claim. Whatever it costs to replace the item today will be the amount you will receive, as long as you *do* replace it.

Let's say your five-year-old camera was stolen. Perhaps you aren't sure whether or not you want to replace it. If you opt for the cash, you will be paid only what a five-year-old camera is worth. If you replace it, you will receive a new camera that is as similar as possible to the one you lost. You cannot replace the item with something better than what you had, or with something different, even if the replacement cost is the same. Similarly, if you decide to replace an item with a cheaper but perhaps more practical one, you are not entitled to the cash for the difference in cost. Insurance is intended to put you back to the way you were before the loss, so replacement cost means just that.

If you're unsure whether or not to replace an item, you can settle for actual cash value and replace it at a later date, as long as this is done within the period allotted for replacement, usually several months.

Whether you are paid actual cash value or replacement cost, you still pay the deductible, unless the item in question has been "scheduled" (see question 13).

50. If an older item that doesn't work anymore is stolen from me, will my insurance company pay to replace it with a new one?

No. Even though you may have replacement cost insurance, some conditions apply. If the item is no longer being used for its original purpose, you will be paid only the actual cash value (a depreciated amount) for it. In other words, insurers will not replace your 15-year-old television set that has been mouldering in the closet with a brand-new one, even if someone *was* stupid enough to steal it! Otherwise, people would expect their insurers to replace all kinds of useless items, and our premiums would skyrocket.

Checklist

Top 10 questions to ask your insurance provider BEFORE you purchase or renew your insurance

1. What kind of homeowners policy do I have, and who/what is covered under it?
2. How do I know if I am adequately insured?
3. What is *not* covered in my homeowners policy? (What are the "exclusions"?)

4. Do I have replacement cost? Guaranteed replacement cost?
5. What are the dollar limitations on valuables, like jewellery, silverware, and computers?
6. What does my policy cover me for in terms of water damage?
7. What optional coverages should I consider?
8. What is my deductible? How much money can I save on my premium by choosing a higher deductible?
9. What safety features can I install that will help me save money and increase my protection?
10. Does the company offer 24-hour claims service?

When you have a claim...

1. Am I covered? For how much? (If not, why not? Show me where in the policy it explains that.)
2. Is there a deductible? How much?
3. Can I get assistance right now to make temporary repairs? How do I go about arranging the repairs?
4. What do I need to do to file my claim as soon as possible?
5. How long will it take to settle my claim?

Keywords

Deductible	the portion of an insurance claim that you agree to pay out of pocket.
Endorsement	(also called a "rider," "floater" or "scheduling") an amendment or extra added to your policy to beef up your coverage. Usually used to provide additional insurance for valuables like jewellery, cameras, furs.
Exclusion	a peril that is not covered under your policy. In other words, it is specifically excluded.
Home insurance	(also called "property" insurance) insurance on your house and its contents, as well as liability protection. *Note:* there are special insurance packages for renters and condominium unit owners.
Peril	something that causes loss or damage, like fire, theft, windstorm.
Personal property	the contents of your home, which are generally covered both at the home and temporarily away from it.
Risk	the chance of a loss.

automobile insurance

What your car insurance covers

How companies decide what to charge for your car insurance

How to save money on your car insurance

How traffic tickets and accidents affect your rating

What to do when you have a claim

Note: This chapter does not contain details on Statutory Accident Benefits (the benefits you receive for medical expenses and income replacement when you are injured in an automobile accident) because these vary considerably from province to province, and can change according to government regulations.

Automobile Insurance:
Don't Leave Home Without It!

U NLIKE OTHER KINDS OF INSURANCE, you don't have a choice about whether or not you buy car insurance: it's the law. Everyone who owns a car must carry a basic level of insurance, but most choose to enhance this package with optional coverages for additional protection.

Car insurance doesn't come cheap, but without it we'd be afraid to set foot outside our homes. One accident could wipe us out financially. Consider the cost to repair or replace your car, loss of income in the event of injuries, and medical expenses not covered by provincial health care, not to mention the possibility of a huge lawsuit from the injured victim if you were at fault. Now imagine if the accident happened in the United States, where hospital costs can run to several thousand dollars a day and lawsuits abound. These costs are covered by your car insurance.

And automobile insurance doesn't just cover the insured person; it protects you and your immediate family as pedestrians or passengers in someone else's car, or even on public transit should a motor vehicle accident occur.

All in all, automobile insurance is a bargain if you are unfortunate enough to need it in the event of a serious accident.

How it works

Insurers consider many factors when deciding what to charge for car insurance. Whereas home insurance can be pretty much what the market will bear, automobile insurance is tightly regulated. In most provinces, automobile insurers must submit their rates for approval to the appropriate regulatory authority. If they want to change their rates—either raise or lower them—they must file an application to do so. Insurers have to be sure their rates are high enough that there will be enough money in their coffers to pay future projected claims. That's where the actuaries—the number crunchers—come in.

Since each insurer pools all its risks, it charges premiums based on all the claims it has paid out for the entire pool. That's why companies are reluctant to insure too many drivers who have had several claims. Studies show that these drivers will probably continue to have more than their share of claims. That will cause rates to increase for all the drivers in the pool.

Provincial authorities also study each company's methods of setting rates and review its underwriting rules—the criteria on which an insurer may decide not to sell auto insurance to a consumer. Since automobile insurance is compulsory, it must be available to everyone who is legally entitled to drive. Although an individual company may refuse to sell you auto insurance if it thinks you're a bad risk, the insurance industry as a whole cannot refuse basic insurance to anybody. But it comes at a price. For high-risk drivers, there are two options: the Facility Association, an industry-sponsored pool of last resort; or so-called "non-standard" insurers, who specialize in insuring high-risk drivers. Either way, you could end up paying as much as a 250-per-cent-surcharge, depending on how many accidents and tickets you've had.

Contrary to popular belief, insurance companies are not raking in big bucks from auto insurance. Many of them lose money on it, while others post only a marginal profit. That's why many insurers will give you a break on your auto insurance premiums if they can supply you the more lucrative home insurance in the bargain.

Since each insurer uses its own criteria for setting rates and classifying risks (subject to approval by provincial authorities where applicable), insurance rates may vary considerably—sometimes as much as $1,000—from one company to the next, even for the same driver and the same coverage. So it pays to shop around for car insurance.

Before you go on your shopping spree, there are a few things to keep in mind. First, the insurance company with the lowest price may not offer the best service come claims time, when you really need it. Likely one of the reasons it can afford to be priced so much lower than its competitors is that it takes a very tough stance at claims time. A company that charges more *may* be more forgiving in settling claims but, like almost everything in insurance, it ain't necessarily so! So, when you're shopping for car insurance, ask friends and colleagues who have had a recent claims experience how they were treated and whether their claim was settled promptly and without hassle.

Insurance companies also tend to favor long-time clients who have good driving records. If you continue to jump from one company to another, you will not be able to take advantage of the premium discounts and other allowances—perhaps forgiveness for an at-fault accident—that often accrue to these customers. Before you switch companies, ask your prospective insurer what impact a minor conviction (like a speeding ticket) and an at-fault accident would have on your rating and, consequently, your premium.

Also keep in mind that car insurance, like every other kind of insurance, is designed to cover major losses that you could not otherwise afford to pay yourself. Insurers judge you by the *number* of claims you make, not by what they have to pay out for each claim. So save your claims for the bigger losses, and swallow the bill for that $300 scratch yourself.

No two provinces alike

Automobile insurance is regulated by each province, so if you move from, say, Nova Scotia to British Columbia, your car insurance will also change. In British Columbia, Saskatchewan, and Manitoba, compulsory auto insurance is provided by a government monopoly, while in other provinces, except Quebec, it is provided by private insurers. In Quebec, insurance for bodily injury or death is provided by a government agency, and the damage to the vehicle itself is covered by private insurers.

Some provinces have "pure no-fault" insurance, meaning that they compensate victims for bodily injury or death only with standard accident benefits; there is no right to sue. Other provinces have a "modified no-fault" system, whereby there may be no right to sue for economic loss, but victims can still sue for pain and suffering, or vice versa. Still other provinces emphasize "tort/liability coverage." In these provinces, accident benefits are relatively small, and so there is no restriction on the right to sue for either pain and suffering or economic loss.

Many people think that "no-fault" insurance means they won't be penalized if they have an accident in which they are found to be at fault. Not so! No-fault insurance doesn't mean that no blame is assigned after a collision; it means that you make all claims from your own insurer, regardless of who is at fault. The advantage of no-fault is that payment to victims of car accidents for injuries is not delayed until blame can be assigned.

Since provincial automobile insurance systems tend to change with the government of the day, we do not discuss accident benefits in this chapter.

Fraud Hall-Of-Shamers—Auto Division

While it's a crying shame how much money is lost to insurance fraud every year (about $1.3 billion), here's a look at the lighter side. These would-be fraudsters, whose gall is surpassed only by their stupidity, are nominees for the Canadian Coalition Against Insurance Fraud's Hall of Shame.

- IGNORANCE IS NOT BLISS: *A man involved in an accident with a telephone pole had not purchased the right coverage, so he said it was a hit-and-run and tried to make a claim. As part of its review of the claim, the insurance company had the vehicle inspected, and knew immediately that he had not been involved in a hit-and-run. The car owner then claimed he didn't understand the policy. Perhaps he should have known more about insurance considering his profession—an insurance salesman.*

- TRADING UP: *One woman hired a thief to make her car "disappear" for the insurance money. But she picked the wrong man for the job. The accomplice liked the car so much better than his own that he kept it. He was later caught driving the car the woman had reported as "stolen," using the vehicle identification number from his old car. You just can't trust a thief anymore.*

- NON-STARTER: *An investigator received a tip that two men were planning to stage a car accident to claim benefits. These partners in crime were surprised when the investigator showed up at the scene of the "accident"—and were truly shocked when she popped the hood of one of the cars. It was missing a key part: the engine. The two men had actually towed one of the cars there to make it look like an accident.*

- DOUBLE JEOPARDY: *For one "accident victim," the camera was a little too candid. When this man claimed he was injured in a car accident, the facts didn't add up for his insurance company. The company decided on video surveillance. Sure enough, the videotape revealed that the man wasn't injured at all. In fact, he was well enough for the camera to catch him stealing a car!*

However, it is very important that you understand this aspect of your automobile insurance, so be sure to ask your insurance provider about it. Some provinces give you the option of increasing your accident benefits and, of course, your premium, according to the weekly income you need to receive in the event of a serious accident. If you are a high-income earner, you will want to ask about this possibility.

While insurance regulations change as you go from one province to the next, your driving record won't; it will follow you wherever you go. If you move from Prince Edward Island to Alberta, the insurer in Alberta will likely check your record before agreeing to cover you.

If you're driving cross-country, you needn't be concerned about the various provincial insurance systems, unless you have an accident en route. Then you will find out that the insurance regulations in the province where you had the accident apply. In other words, if you are injured in a car accident in a province where pure no-fault insurance applies, you will not be able to sue the driver who hit you, even though you might have that right in your own province. Of course, the reverse would also hold true. We're not suggesting you bone up on the auto insurance systems for each province before you embark on your cross-country vacation. That would be going above and beyond your obligations as a responsible insurance consumer. On the other hand, if you have trouble sleeping at night, that research might be just the ticket.

The Way It Was

Unearthed from the archives of Canadian Insurance *magazine, a national trade publication founded in 1905.*

Some Things Never Change...

"Loss of autos by theft—especially of Ford cars—are increasing. Forty per cent of such cars are not recovered."
—Canadian Insurance, 1914

"The Toronto chief of Police advises all motor owners to lock their cars before leaving them standing on the street. He says the department has been giving much time and attention to the matter of auto thefts and quite a number of special police with cycles and cars to trace the stolen autos. In spite of these efforts, the evil has not been evaded, and it is up to the owners to do their part. It may become necessary to make the locking of standing cars compulsory."
—Canadian Insurance, 1920

...But Female Drivers Gain Respect!

Author's note: In a lengthy article titled "Salient Points in Automobile Underwriting," author Roy H. Sloan cited such factors as nationality(!), "the habits and personal life of the applicant," and this zinger:
"Age and Sex—Under this heading, the company is anxious to know whether the car is being driven by a minor or a woman. Experience shows that both these types are poor risks, the first on account of careless and reckless driving, and the latter because of nervous and excitable temperament."
—Canadian Insurance, 1925

[Author's note: *Female drivers are now considered the better risks!*]

Frequently Asked Questions ...
About Automobile Insurance

1. Do I have to have automobile insurance, even if my car is not worth much?

Yes, it's the law in Canada. If you drive a car, you must have insurance. Otherwise, your licence may be suspended and you will face a hefty fine— as much as $5,000 for a first offence, up to $50,000 for repeat convictions, depending on the law in your province. Without insurance, if you are injured in an accident, even if it wasn't your fault, you are not entitled to any of the benefits that insurance pays to accident victims. And if you *were* at fault in an accident, you could be sued by the injured victim(s). You would have to pay for your defence, as well as any awards that were made against you, out of your own pocket. That would add up to a lot more than the cost of replacing your aging car.

2. Who sells car insurance?

There are plenty of options. You can buy your car insurance from a broker, agent, or direct-response insurer, as well as through a group plan. A broker represents several different insurance companies; an agent represents only the company that employs him or her; and a direct-response insurer sells its own insurance via telephone. Group insurance is sold through one's workplace, alumni association, professional association, or other group affiliation. You can even buy car insurance over the Internet, but it must still be sold through a licensed agent, broker, or direct-response insurer. (See chapter 1 for more details on how insurance is sold.)

If you live in a province where the government has a monopoly on selling basic insurance—British Columbia, Saskatchewan, Manitoba, and Quebec—you must purchase your insurance through a broker who has been authorized by the government to sell automobile insurance on its behalf. You can still purchase additional, optional coverage (see question 5) from a private insurer, however, through a broker, agent, or direct-response insurer licensed to sell insurance in your province.

3. How do I choose an insurance company? Is all insurance the same?

Since auto insurance is regulated, the basic policy sold by each insurer must be the same. However, it pays to shop around, as prices vary considerably from company to company, even for the same coverage. That's because each company has its own system for classifying risks and setting rates (see "How it works," page 64).

Therefore, prices may differ, not only on the basic mandatory coverage that is required in each province (see question 4), but also on optional coverages, like Collision, Comprehensive, and special endorsements, or "add ons," you may request (see question 5). Some companies may not offer certain endorsements, like "waiver of depreciation" (see question 56).

Claims service also varies from company to company. Some insurers have a reputation for paying claims promptly and efficiently, while others seem to forget that they're in the business of paying claims at all. Often, the company with the cheapest rates is not the most accommodating at claims time; that's why it is able to charge less than most of its competitors. Ask friends and relatives what company they are insured with, and how it handled any claims they had. Ask your provincial regulator if it has conducted any surveys on claims satisfaction; Ontario, for one, has published a claims satisfaction survey that it distributes to consumers (see "Consumer Resources" in Appendix A for a list of provincial regulators).

If you are buying auto insurance from a broker, find out which insurance companies the broker represents. Then ask the broker to explain the differences, as well as show you quotes from each company in which you are interested. Ask how each company treats one at-fault accident (see question 15). (For more questions to ask your insurance provider, see the Checklist at the end of this chapter.)

Caution: Don't switch insurance companies at the drop of a hat—or a premium—without considering all the implications (see question 47).

4. What does my car insurance include?

Basic mandatory car insurance generally includes:

- *Statutory Accident Benefits*—pay for your medical expenses and provide you with income replacement (up to a certain limit) if you are injured or killed in an accident, regardless of who was at fault. These benefits also apply if you, or a member of your household, are injured as a pedestrian or cyclist. Accident benefit features vary widely from one province to the next.
- *Third-Party Liability* (minimum usually $200,000)—pays for losses you cause others while driving; for example, if you injure someone or damage someone else's property and they sue you. This coverage pays for your legal defence, if needed, as well as any damages awarded in lawsuits against you, up to the limit of your coverage. Many consumers choose to extend their coverage to at least $1 million. Otherwise, you would be on the hook for any damages/legal costs above $200,000 if you were found legally liable for a claim.
- *Uninsured Automobile Coverage*—pays for injury to you or your passengers caused by an uninsured or a hit-and-run driver, subject to a certain limit. *Note:* This insurance does not cover damage to your *automobile* caused by a hit-and-run driver. For that to be covered, you need to carry optional Collision or All Perils insurance (see questions 5 and 13).

There may be other coverages included with your basic mandatory car insurance, depending on the province in which you live. Check with your insurance provider.

5. What kinds of optional coverage should I consider?

- *Collision*—pays to fix or replace your car (whichever is most economical) if it's damaged in a collision, even if you're at fault. It also pays if your car was damaged by a driver who was not insured or identified (see question 13). *Note:* If you have a long history of at-fault accidents, the insurer may refuse to sell you Collision coverage—or any coverage at all!
- *Comprehensive*—pays for the repair or replacement of your car due to a non-collision loss, like theft (except by a member of your household), fire, lightning, hail, windstorm, earthquake, impact with animals, falling objects, rising water, vandalism, and explosion. You may choose "Specified

Perils" coverage instead, but this covers only the causes of damage listed in the policy, and does not usually include vandalism or damage to windshields caused by flying rocks.

- *Extended Third-Party Liability*—increases your liability coverage from the basic mandatory amount (usually $200,000) to at least $1 million (see question 4).
- *Other endorsements*, like "waiver of depreciation" (see question 56), "loss of use" coverage to pay for a rental car if your car is being repaired as the result of an accident, and coverage for damage to a rented or borrowed vehicle (see question 25), to name a few.

Ask your insurance provider about other options, including any that pertain to accident benefits, as this coverage varies from one province to the next.

6. How do insurance companies decide what to charge for car insurance?

Insurance companies price insurance according to variables called "risk factors." These include:

- *Where you drive*—Like many other things, car insurance is usually cheaper in the country than in the city, simply because you are more likely to be involved in an accident if you're driving in a high-traffic area. The difference in price could be as much as $200.
- *How far you drive*—Since your chances of being in an accident increase the more you drive, people who use their car for business and who commute long distances to and from work pay more for insurance than those who drive shorter distances or only for pleasure (not to work). If you're changing jobs and want to estimate the full cost of commuting that extra distance, figure in a higher premium along with additional wear and tear.
- *The kind of car you drive*—Most insurers are now using the CLEAR (Canadian Loss Experience Automobile Rating) system of rating vehicles for insurance purposes. That means they take into account a vehicle model's claims experience when they calculate your premium, rather than using the manufacturer's suggested list price, as was done in the past. In other words, vehicle models that cost more to repair, have fewer safety features, or are stolen more often cost more to insure (see ques-

tions 11 and 12). Before you buy a car, ask your insurance provider if your insurance company uses the CLEAR system (eventually, almost all companies will) and, if so, what the rating is for the model you're considering.

- *Your age, sex, and marital status*—So much for being innocent until proven guilty. When it comes to pricing insurance, the law of averages prevails, and it's perfectly legal for insurers to set prices based on age, sex, and even marital status. Accident rates are higher for drivers under age 25 than for older, more experienced drivers; higher for young males than for young females; and higher for young, single males than young, married ones (see question 36). Therefore, if you're young, male, and single, you're going to take a big hit in the wallet—as much as two to three times what an older driver is charged. (Passing an accredited driver education course will lop about $200 off the total in the first year of driving.) Conversely, older drivers often get a discount on their premiums. While this may not seem fair to young people, especially those who haven't had any claims, the alternative would be to raise everyone's premiums to subsidize the heavy losses sustained by these drivers. You can just imagine how popular *that* decision would be!

- *Your driving record*—If you have at-fault accidents or driving convictions (speeding tickets, seatbelt infractions, or other moving violations) on your record, you will pay considerably more for your insurance than someone who has been accident- and conviction-free for several years. Various studies have proven that, if you already have had an at-fault accident and a few speeding tickets, you stand a better chance, statistically, of being in another accident than does a driver with a spotless record. Most insurance companies assign their insured drivers a rating up to six—and sometimes seven or ten—stars. To stay at the top level, and pay the least for your insurance, you can usually have no more than one minor conviction in a three-year period. Otherwise, you drop to a lower classification and you'll be charged more for your insurance (see questions 15, 16, and 17). In some provinces, your rating may also be affected if the insurer has to pay several claims on your behalf, even if they weren't your fault, as in a Comprehensive claim, for example (see question 19).

- *Your coverage*—While basic insurance is mandatory (see question 4), there are many optional coverages (see question 5) you can purchase that would affect your premium, as would the deductibles you choose on those coverages (see question 8).

- *Any discounts for which you are eligible* (see question 7).
- *Who else will be driving your car*—your spouse, a child under the age of 25, etc. You will pay more if your 20-year-old son or your spouse whose nickname is "Crash" is driving your car (see question 46).

You will also be charged more for auto insurance if you've ever had your policy cancelled for not providing correct or complete information on your application, or for failing to pay your premium (see question 24).

Remember, each insurance company maintains its own classification system and sets its own underwriting rules, so rates may vary considerably from one company to another, even for a driver with the same risk profile (see "How it works" on page 64).

7. How can I save money on my car insurance?

There are several ways in which you can save money on your automobile insurance, without compromising your coverage:

- Consider choosing a higher deductible. The higher your deductible, the lower the premium you will pay. However, don't choose such a high deductible that you couldn't pay it out of pocket if you had to (see question 8).
- For young and new drivers, take a driver training course from an approved school. That can boost you from a "zero" rating (for less than one year of accident-free driving) to as high as a three-star rating (for three years of accident-free driving) in one fell swoop, saving you as much as 40 per cent on your insurance. Some insurers even give discounts to young drivers with good grades.
- Choose a car whose claims experience is good. Many insurers now take this into account when pricing insurance. Generally, a newer-model, family-style car has a better claims record than a sports model or a sport-utility vehicle (see questions 6, 11, and 12).
- Drive as safely as possible. Of all the risk factors insurers take into account when calculating your premium, your driving record likely has the greatest impact. Maintaining an accident- and conviction-free record is the most effective way to keep insurance costs to a minimum.

- Consider placing all your insurance with one company. Insurers may give you a discount of up to 15 per cent if you place both your property and automobile insurance with them. They may also give you a discount— usually anywhere from 5 to 20 per cent—if you are a long-time client with a good driving record.
- Take advantage of any other discounts that may be offered, such as: multi-car, mature driver, low mileage, and installation of theft-prevention devices. Depending on the insurer, one or more of these could bring down your insurance premium by 5 to 15 per cent.
- Inform your insurance provider of any changes in your circumstances that would improve your risk profile and reduce your premium accordingly: if you move to a less populated area; if you change jobs and commute fewer miles to work; if you buy a new car that may have a better insurance rating; if you start a home business and no longer drive to work; if you reduce the number of drivers in your household.
- Don't make small claims—it will cost you more in the long run (see question 51). Better to swallow the cost yourself. That goes for claims under your Comprehensive insurance too. Although insurance companies are not supposed to penalize you for these types of claims, don't count on it. Make one too many, and you could find yourself with a whopping deductible, or no Comprehensive coverage at all (see question 19).
- Check out group plans at your workplace, professional or alumni association, auto club, etc. You may be able to save some money by taking advantage of a group rate.

If you drive an older, low-value car, you might want to consider dropping your Collision and Comprehensive coverage. If you do, however, be prepared to pay out of pocket to repair or replace your vehicle if you are hit by an unidentified driver, even if you weren't at fault (see question 13).

Finally, keep in mind that the cheapest company may not be the best at claims time. Don't make price your only consideration (see Checklist at the end of this chapter).

8. How do I decide what deductible to choose?

If you make a claim under your optional Collision, Comprehensive, or Named Perils coverage, or under your mandatory Uninsured Automobile coverage, you must pay a deductible—the amount of the claim you must pay before your insurance kicks in. In other words, if your claim is for $2,000 and your deductible is $500, you would pay $500 and the insurance company would pay $1,500. Deductibles may range from as low as $100 to more than $2,000, depending on the type of coverage you have and the province in which you live. Most companies have a minimum deductible, but you can choose a higher one in order to save money on your premium. The higher the deductible, the lower your premium. This could make a significant difference in the case of a young male driver, for example, who is charged a high rate for Collision coverage.

In choosing a deductible, make sure you select an amount that you could afford to pay out of pocket if you were involved in an accident tomorrow. If you wouldn't be comfortable shelling out $1,000 or even $500, choose a lower amount, even though you will end up paying a higher premium. Ask yourself: How much of the claim am I willing to pay in order to get a lower premium?

A brochure published by the Financial Services Commission of Ontario (which regulates insurance in that province), called "Shopping for Car Insurance," illustrates typical savings that would result from a higher deductible. On Collision insurance, for example, increasing your deductible from $300 to $500 would save you only about $38 a year on average, while raising your Comprehensive deductible from $100 to $300 would put an extra $29 or so a year in your pocket. At that rate, it would take more than six years of paying premiums at the lower rate to make up for the $200 you

TIP

Buyer Beware!

Before you buy a new—or used—car, ask your insurance provider which makes and models cost less to insure. Or get a copy of the brochures "How Cars Measure Up" or "Choosing Your Car" from the Vehicle Information Centre of Canada and check for yourself (see Appendix A for contact information).

would save if you had an accident and paid the lower deductible. The choice is yours.

Before choosing a deductible, ask your insurance provider what the difference in premium would be with a higher deductible versus a lower one, and make your decision accordingly.

Depending on the regulations in your province, you may be able to recover all or part of your deductible for Collision coverage, if you were not at fault or only partially at fault in an accident.

9. If I have an anti-theft device in my automobile, like a car alarm, will my premium be lower?

That should be taken into account when the insurer calculates your premium. While there are many other factors that dictate how much you pay for your insurance (see question 6), loss-prevention equipment and other safety features will be looked upon favourably by insurers. Savings may be in the range of $30, depending on the location of the vehicle, the type of vehicle, and the type of theft-deterrent device—alarm, steering-wheel locking bars, engine cut-off system, or electronic immobilization. (Electronic immobilization, generally considered the most effective, means your ignition key is electronically coded, so the vehicle will not start without your key.)

To find out which anti-theft devices are standard or optional on each vehicle make and model, order a copy of the brochure "Choosing Your Car," available free from the Vehicle Information Centre of Canada, a non-profit industry organization that compiles claims information (see "Consumer Resources" in Appendix A for contact information).

10. If I don't use my car during the winter, can I get a reduction on my premium?

Ask your insurance provider about arranging an endorsement that will suspend your Third-Party Liability and Collision coverage for the period of time you are not driving your car. (This endorsement is referred to by different names, depending on the province in which you live.) Make sure your Accident Benefits coverage continues (in case you're injured while a passenger in someone else's car or as a pedestrian), as well as your

Comprehensive coverage (against theft, fire, vandalism, etc.), while the car is in storage.

11. Why doesn't my insurance get cheaper as my car gets older? Isn't the price of my premium based on the value of my automobile?

Not anymore, at least as far as most insurers are concerned. Most insurance companies these days use the CLEAR (Canadian Loss Experience Automobile Rating) system instead of the manufacturer's suggested retail price as a basis for calculating the cost of your insurance. CLEAR rates each model according to its road performance and claims history. Therefore, safety features, such as air bags, anti-lock brakes, and anti-theft devices that can add substantially to the price of a vehicle may translate into lower premiums for car owners, since these devices also help curb insurers' claim costs.

Before CLEAR was introduced (to much acclaim by consumer groups), insurers simply paid the collision repair costs and passed them on to everyone in the policyholder's rate class. To illustrate, let's say you and your neighbour each had a car that cost $25,000. According to the previous system, both cars would be rated the same for insurance purposes. Yet, one car gets stolen much more frequently than the other one, is involved in more collisions, and costs more to repair. Is it fair to charge each car owner the same amount for insurance? With the CLEAR system, motorists with safer vehicles that are less expensive to insure do not subsidize those with higher loss costs. CLEAR also helps encourage automakers to build vehicles that are safer, less damage-prone, and more theft-resistant, and rewards consumers for buying them.

You can check the claims rating for each vehicle model in the brochures "Choosing Your Car" and "How Cars Measure Up," both published by the Vehicle Information Centre of Canada, a non-profit industry organization that compiles claims information (see "Consumer Resources" in Appendix A for contact information). "Choosing Your Car" outlines the availability of air bags, anti-lock brakes, and theft-deterrent devices on cars and light trucks for the latest model-year available, and offers comparative insurance rankings of cars and light trucks for the past five model years; "How Cars

Measure Up" shows the insurance claims experience of the most popular Canadian models of cars, passenger vans, sport-utility vehicles, and pickup trucks for the latest model-year available (usually about two years behind the current model-year). It's a good idea to check this information when you're buying a used car, or ask your insurance provider how the model you are considering ranks in the claims department (if your insurer is using that system). You might be surprised (see question 12). A similar rating system is now available for motorcycles as well.

Of course, the type of car you drive is only one variable that is thrown into the mix to determine the price of your insurance. There are several other so-called "risk factors" that influence the cost, such as where you live, how far you drive, how often you drive, your age, and your driving record (see question 6).

Those factors aside, there are other reasons why your insurance costs continue to climb even as your car depreciates. Like just about everything else, the cost of car repairs, medical care, and other services we need when we're in a car accident escalates year after year, and we all pay the price in our premiums. Like it or not, that's how insurance works; the payments of many cover the losses of a few.

12. Why do I pay more for my insurance than my neighbour does, even though he has a newer, more expensive car?

Your insurance doesn't necessarily get cheaper as your car gets older, but there could be several reasons why your neighbour pays less. First, most insurance companies now use the CLEAR (Canadian Loss Experience Automobile Rating) system to rate vehicles for insurance purposes. CLEAR rates cars on their road performance and claims history, rather than their initial cost (see question 11).

That means your five-year-old Honda Civic might cost more to insure than your neighbour's spanking-new Ford Taurus. Because your older car has fewer safety features than your neighbour's newer model, the insurer reasons, it is more likely to be involved in an accident, and you are more likely to be injured if this unfortunate event does occur. It might cost more to fix the damage on your car, since automakers are now trying to build vehicles with parts that do not cost as much to repair and replace (some have succeeded; some haven't). Your car might also be more prone to theft, since it doesn't come equipped with the latest anti-theft devices like your neighbour's car does.

The worst offenders, from a claims standpoint, are two-door high-performance sports cars and sport-utility vehicles. While sports cars are more likely to be involved in collisions (including those in which personal injuries are sustained), sport-utility vehicles are favourite targets for thieves. At the other end of the spectrum, station wagons are the least likely to be stolen (no surprise there), followed by other four-door family models. So if you want to save money on your insurance, flashy is not the way to go. Get a copy of the brochure "Choosing Your Car" from the Vehicle Information Centre of Canada (see "Consumer Resources" in Appendix A for contact information) to assess how your particular model stacks up.

As companies gradually convert to the CLEAR system, some policyholders may find their premiums increasing, while others will get a reduction. Insurers are supposed to transfer costs from cars that are cheaper to insure to those that are more expensive to insure; they should not be taking in more money as a result of the conversion to CLEAR.

The CLEAR system is only one reason why your neighbour might be paying less for insurance than you are. He may also have fewer optional coverages than you do, a better driving record, and higher deductible payments. Or he may drive his car shorter distances. All these factors can have an impact on the cost of your insurance (see question 6). Finally, prices can vary considerably from one insurance company to another, even if all the other variables are exactly the same. Different companies have different rate structures.

13. If I have an older car, do I need Collision insurance?

That's a decision only you can make, perhaps with some input from your insurance provider. If your car is very old, you might want to consider dropping Collision and/or Comprehensive coverages (both are optional). But before you do, think about whether the money you will save on your premium justifies the risk of having to foot the entire bill for repairing or replacing your vehicle if it is damaged—your fault or not.

Also consider that, if your car is damaged in a hit-and-run accident, the only way for insurance to pay for that damage is through your Collision coverage. If you don't carry Collision insurance, you will be stuck with the entire bill for an accident that wasn't even your fault. Your only other recourse would be to track down and recover the money yourself from the driver who hit you—a challenge for even the most intrepid P.I. And don't look to your insurance company to help you. You're on your own.

Finally, if you lease your car or you have taken out a bank loan to buy it, you don't have a choice about whether or not you carry Collision coverage—you have to.

14. If I have an accident that was not my fault, will my insurance rates still go up?

No, they shouldn't. That's the theory, anyway. In actual practice, they might, especially if you had a series of such accidents. And too many Comprehensive claims could result in the company refusing to sell you this kind of coverage anymore (see question 19).

15. If I have been driving many years without a claim, but have an accident in which I am at fault, will my rates go up? How long does the accident stay on my record?

More than likely, your premium will go up if you have an accident in which you were at fault, either completely or partially. Some insurance companies will "forgive" one at-fault accident, particularly if you are a long-term customer with an otherwise good record. If your insurer doesn't believe in forgiveness, it will lower your rating by one star, and maybe even more. Count on paying at least 15 to 20 per cent more as a result.

Your chances of being forgiven are much less if you are a new client, or if your insurer's prices are significantly lower than its competitors (the insurer maintains its price advantage by taking a hard line at claims time). That's why you should think twice before switching companies in order to save a few bucks on your premium—it could cost you more in the long run. Ask what the new company's forgiveness policy is for an at-fault accident before you make your decision.

An at-fault accident stays on your driving record for as many years as it takes to requalify for the best driving level—six years for six stars, seven years for seven stars, and so on, even if you move to another province. If

The Fast Lane To A Higher Premium

Q. You receive your second speeding ticket in two years. Will it affect your insurance premium?

A. Probably, if the insurance company finds out about it. While it might forgive one ticket, a second ticket in a two-year period would likely prompt your insurer to drop you to a lower rating level and charge you a higher premium—perhaps as much as 20 per cent. However, unless the insurer has a reason to check your Motor Vehicle Record (MVR)—if you have an accident or are applying for insurance elsewhere—your tickets might go unnoticed.

you apply for insurance with another company, you will be asked on the application if you have had any accidents in the last six years and, if so, whether you were found to be at fault in any way.

16. What happens if I have more than one at-fault accident?

Get ready to pay through the nose! If you have a good record with your insurance company, it may forgive one at-fault accident, but certainly not two in the space of three years. Your premiums will go up considerably as a result, probably at least 25 per cent; or the company may even choose not to renew your coverage. You will have to seek insurance elsewhere, and pay an exorbitant rate to get it. When one company in the regular insurance market refuses to insure you, the rest usually follow suit. That leaves you with only one solution: a company that specializes in insuring high-risk drivers, like the Facility Association or one of the so-called "non-standard" insurers. You'll pay a huge surcharge until you can "earn" your way back into the regular market by maintaining a spotless driving record for a specified period of time—at least a few years.

Finding Fault

Q. You are driving in a blinding rainstorm, when all of a sudden you see a car stopped in the lane ahead. You slam on your brakes, but too late—you rear-end it, causing damage to both cars. The police officer who comes to the scene says you won't be charged because of the weather conditions. But will the accident affect your insurance?

A. Yes. You would be held at fault by the insurance company because you hit the other car. Insurance companies decide whether or not you are at fault in an accident based on regulations set out in the provincial Insurance Acts. These "fault determination rules" are not related to charges laid—or not laid—by police. There is no allowance for poor road conditions or other extenuating circumstances.

17. Do I get penalized on my insurance for speeding tickets or seat-belt tickets? How does the insurance company find out if I have received any tickets?

Most insurance companies will forgive one minor moving violation, like a speeding ticket (less than 30 km/h over the limit) or seat-belt ticket, but they are unlikely to overlook two in a three-year period. If you want to stay at the highest rating level, and pay the least for your insurance, you can't have more than one moving violation in a three-year period. Otherwise, you drop to a lower classification and pay anywhere from 5 to 20 per cent more for your insurance. A third conviction in three years could mean an increase in your insurance premium of at least 25 per cent. It might even oust you from the regular insurance market and force you into the so-called "high-risk" market where you could pay as much as 250 per cent more for your insurance (see question 16).

However, unless you are applying for insurance at another company, or your current insurance company happens to do a random check on your

Motor Vehicle Record (MVR) (which it might be more inclined to do if you were involved in an accident), it is unlikely that a moving violation would come to light—a good reason for sticking with your current insurer.

A moving violation stays on your MVR for two years. However, if you are applying for insurance at another company, you will be asked whether you have had any tickets in the last three years (see questions 21 and 22).

18. Do I get penalized if my car is stolen?

Not if the car was definitely stolen (and doesn't simply "disappear" after you gave permission to someone else to drive it). Theft claims are covered under your Comprehensive insurance, if you have that coverage. There is no deductible payable on claims involving a stolen car or a total loss due to fire, and you should not be penalized on your insurance premium for making a claim. However, as usual in the insurance world, there is a proviso. If you have too many Comprehensive claims, the insurer might refuse to sell you Comprehensive coverage (see question 19). If this happens to you, offer to take a very high deductible without the usual reduction in premium that goes along with it. That will reduce the company's risk and may encourage the insurer to reconsider its decision. It also helps your case if the company insures your home as well. Finally, be willing to implement any loss-prevention measures that could deter car thieves, like installing a car alarm, keeping your car in the garage, etc.—a good idea under any circumstance.

19. If I have claims under my Comprehensive insurance, will my rates go up?

They shouldn't. Comprehensive claims are not considered at-fault accidents. Remember, rates increase because of fault, not because of the money paid out by the insurance company to settle a claim. However, you should be aware that, although insurers in certain provinces cannot raise your rates or cancel your automobile policy because of Comprehensive claims, they can raise the deductible on your Comprehensive coverage, or even delete that coverage altogether if the company thinks you have had more than your share of these kinds of claims (see question 18). In other provinces, they might even refuse to renew your entire auto policy as a result of frequent Comprehensive claims. Although Comprehensive losses are not your fault, insurers believe that these kinds of claims can, to a certain extent, be controlled. By taking a hard line, they figure they can prod you into taking the necessary precautions to prevent some of these claims from recurring (a car that is broken into repeatedly for its stereo equipment, for example).

You may want to consider paying for smaller losses yourself, instead of claiming on your Comprehensive coverage. Keep in mind that it's the *frequency* of claims, and not their total value, that counts most in the eyes of insurers. You're better off making one $10,000 claim than three $1,000 claims (see question 51).

So don't think that you have carte blanche with Comprehensive claims. Even though, in most cases, Comprehensive claims are beyond your control, they still go on your insurance record.

20. What happens if I'm charged with impaired driving?

Impaired driving, like negligent driving causing death, is considered a "serious" conviction on your driving record (as opposed to a speeding ticket, which counts as a minor conviction). A serious conviction will expel you from the regular insurance market and force you into a special insurance pool called "Facility Association" for drivers who are considered high risk. In Facility, you will be surcharged at least 100 per cent, and possibly up to 250 per cent if you have other convictions as well, for your insurance. You have to earn your way out of Facility by maintaining a claims- and conviction-free driving record for at least two years. You could also seek insurance with one of the non-standard companies that specialize in insuring so-called high-risk drivers. There are several of these companies in Canada. Their rates may be cheaper than those of the Facility Association, but definitely much higher than you would be charged in the standard market.

Not only will you pay a lot more for your insurance in the future, but your insurance company will not cover any damage to your vehicle if you were impaired and at fault in an accident. You may also not be entitled to certain accident benefits. A drinking-and-driving conviction can stay on your driver's record for 10 years.

21. How long do I have to go back in reporting an accident or traffic ticket on my insurance application?

Generally, you will be asked for details of any accident or claim during the last six years (including claims under your Comprehensive coverage, like theft, windshield damage, etc.). You will also be asked about your conviction record in the last three years. This includes any offences relating to the operation of your car, like speeding tickets, seat-belt infractions, or other moving violations. You can obtain your Motor Vehicle Record (MVR) for the last two years from the Ministry of Transportation, but insurance companies require a three-year history. Therefore, if you are not sure of conviction or accident dates, ask your current insurance provider.

It's a good idea to keep a record of the dates of any tickets, accidents, or claims, because how many of us can remember if that minor accident happened six years ago or seven? It makes a difference to the insurer (see question 22).

22. What if I say on my insurance application that I don't have any traffic convictions, even though I do? It's easy to forget about a speeding ticket, or how long ago my last accident was.

Sometimes we really would like to forget about that annoying ticket we received. But that's not a good idea, at least as far as your insurance applica-

CAUTION

Sharpen Your Memory

When applying for insurance, don't "forget"—conveniently or otherwise—to tell the insurer about that speeding ticket you got two years ago. The company will find out anyway when it checks your Motor Vehicle Record (MVR). If you really aren't sure about the dates of the tickets you received, better to say you don't remember than to get caught in a white lie.

tion is concerned. If you're not sure of the date of your last ticket or accident, tell your prospective insurer you can't remember when it was. If you say you haven't had any tickets in the last three years and the insurer discovers otherwise—and it will—it may refuse your application or charge you more for your coverage.

Any inaccuracies or omissions in your policy, intentional or not, could result in your policy being declared invalid. That means that if you had a claim, it would not be paid and your insurance could be cancelled or deemed never to have been in force (see question 24). Once you have been cancelled, replacing your coverage will cost you a bundle.

If you are providing information over the phone to a broker, agent, or call centre representative who is filling out the application on your behalf, you are still responsible for its contents, even if the insurance representative makes a mistake. Make sure you read the policy carefully before you sign it.

23. If I say I do not drive my car to work, but then take it one day because of an appointment and have an accident, will the insurance company still pay my claim?

Don't worry. Insurance companies do make some allowances for circumstances like this. As long as driving to work was an exception, the company should pay your claim.

24. Can the company cancel my car insurance? If so, under what circumstances?

Yes, they can, generally for two main reasons:
- *Non-payment of premiums.* Your insurance premium is due as soon as you receive the bill. If you don't pay it, your insurer will cancel your coverage, plain and simple. So don't let your payment go into arrears! If you can't pay the premium as promised, contact your insurance provider before the account is considered delinquent and a solution may be reached. Another important point: If you have decided to switch insurers at renewal time, don't think that simply ignoring your renewal notice will terminate your agreement with your previous insurer. You must notify the insurer in writing of your intention not to renew; otherwise, you are still committed to that insurance and on the hook for the payment.

How Do You Rate?

Q. You say on your insurance application that you drive your car only for pleasure. However, a few months later, you start driving to work. Do you have to tell the insurance company?
A. Yes. Insurers calculate your premium based on a number of risk factors. One of them is how you use your car. If you start driving to work every day rather than just for pleasure, your rating will change and your premium will go up. But if you don't tell your insurer that you're driving to work every day (and how far) and you have an accident, your claim may be denied.

• *Inaccuracies or omissions in your application, intentional or not.* Even if your insurance provider has filled in your application form for you, over the telephone, for example, you are still responsible for the accuracy of that information.

The insurer could also cancel your insurance if you didn't report a change in the risk—for example, you start using your car to deliver pizza, while your insurer thinks it is being driven for pleasure only.

Having your insurance cancelled is inconvenient enough, but it gets worse. The cancellation will appear as a black mark on your insurance record that will follow you as you scramble to find coverage elsewhere—at an inflated premium, thanks to your now-blemished record.

The insurer must give you 15 days' notice by registered mail, or five days' written notice personally delivered, of the cancellation. The 15 days begin on the day following the receipt of the registered letter at the post office to which it is addressed. *Note:* It doesn't matter whether or not you have picked up the registered letter; as long as it has been *delivered* to the post office, the clock is ticking.

The insurer must also refund you any excess of premium paid if it cancels your insurance. In other words, if you paid for one year's insurance and your insurance was cancelled after eight months, the insurer would refund you the money for the four months you had remaining on your policy.

Note: There is a difference between cancellation and non-renewal. Cancellation of your insurance could take place at any time during the coverage period, usually for the reasons listed above; non-renewal means the insurer chooses not to renew your coverage at the end of its term. This could be for a number of reasons, but most likely because you have had too many claims and the insurer considers you a poor risk.

25. When I rent a car, should I take the insurance that the rental agency offers? What about credit cards that include insurance on rental cars?

Your Canadian insurance coverage will most likely protect you against injuries you might cause to others, and other property that you might damage with the rental car (make sure you are carrying enough liability coverage!), as well as provide accident benefits if you are injured. However, it doesn't cover damage to the rental car itself, so that's why you need additional insurance. However, there is a cheaper way to insure your rental car than forking out the approximately $12 to $15 a day that car rental agencies charge for what they call "collision damage waiver." Actually, collision damage waiver isn't insurance at all—it's really just a buy-down on the deductible of the agency's own policy, because the agency already has its own insurance on the vehicle. And this waiver may come with some conditions attached; for example, it may apply only to collision damage and not to claims caused by fire or theft; if that's the case, the renter could still be liable if the car was stolen. It might also exclude coverage for damage caused by a collision with a stationary object, like a low-hanging overhead beam in a parking garage, or when the damage occurs off-road.

You can avoid most of these pitfalls, and save yourself some money, by asking your insurance provider to add a "27 endorsement," or "rental vehicle insurance" (it may have different names depending on the province) to your car insurance policy. This provides you with coverage for damage to non-owned automobiles, like a rental car, in Canada and the United States (ask your insurance provider or travel agent about coverage if you are driving internationally), for both the person signing the rental agreement and his or her spouse. The rental agreement must be in the name of the insured person named on the auto policy. That means if two friends are sharing the same rental car, they each need to add this endorsement to their own auto policies. This generally costs only about $25 a year, so it pays for itself within a couple of days of renting the car, if you consider how quickly the cost of the collision damage waiver adds up. It might even offer you broader coverage.

The only potential downside to the 27 endorsement is that, if you did have an at-fault accident with the rental car, it would count against your driving record, since your insurance company would pay the claim. With the rental agency's insurance, you can simply get the car replaced and carry on without a lot of fuss and bother.

Some credit cards offer collision damage waiver coverage if you use the card to pay for the car rental. But this option comes with a fistful of caveats. First, make sure the card still offers that coverage. Some cards that previously offered it no longer do. Next, check who is covered under the insurance; it may be only the cardholder, leaving the spouse or other potential drivers without coverage. There is probably a time limitation as well. Finally, remember that, because you have rejected the offer of insurance from the car rental firm, you will have to negotiate with the credit card company for any claims payments. You might even have to pay for any damage upfront, and then collect from your credit card company later, as the rental company will want the car fixed immediately.

Note: If you are renting the car because your own car was damaged in an accident and is in for repairs, and if you have the "loss of use" endorsement

---

TIP

Protect Your Assets

Make sure you are carrying enough liability coverage. The minimum requirement is usually $200,000, but consider boosting your coverage to at least $1 million—just in case. This is especially important if you are driving in the United States, where lawsuits are commonplace and settlements are in U.S. dollars.

that provides you with a rental car, your own Collision coverage will remain in effect (assuming you carry this insurance).

26. Is there a policy to cover drivers who don't own their own automobile but often drive other vehicles, such as rental cars or friends' vehicles?

There is a policy called a "driver's policy" that insures the driver, rather than the vehicle. However, not all insurers offer it, so you may have to shop around to find one that does. It may be expensive, however, because it must take into account the many different types of vehicles that could possibly be driven.

27. Does my insurance cover me for driving in the United States? What about Mexico?

Your insurance in Canada covers you for driving anywhere in the United States (including Hawaii and Alaska), but not Mexico. If you are planning to drive in Mexico, you will need to buy insurance coverage from a licensed Mexican insurance company. Check with your insurance provider or travel agent before you go.

If you're heading to the U.S. for a vacation (less than six months), you're under no obligation to inform your insurance provider before you leave, but it's not a bad idea, just to find out what the claims procedure would be if you had an accident while you were away (see question 28). Also make sure

CAUTION

Insurance Stops At Mexico

Don't drive in Mexico without buying insurance from a licensed Mexican insurance company. Although your Canadian auto insurance is valid throughout the U.S., resist the urge to slip over the border to Tijuana for a tequila unless you've arranged for special coverage or you leave your car behind.

that your insurance doesn't expire while you're gone, and that you're carrying enough liability insurance. Remember, any lawsuits filed against you there would be payable in U.S. dollars, and payouts for personal injury lawsuits can be hefty in some states.

28. What happens if I have an accident while driving in the U.S.?

Generally, your insurance company would appoint an independent adjuster who lives in the area where the accident took place to handle your claim. If your insurance company also operates in the U.S., it might use one of its own staff. If that is the case, the company may already have provided you with contact names and numbers. Look on your policy and your pink liability slip, or ask your insurance provider.

If you are injured in the U.S. and want to launch a lawsuit against the at-fault driver, there are no restrictions to doing so, since the law that applies is the law of the state where the accident occurred. Therefore, not only can you take advantage of the accident benefits available through your own insurance company, you can also launch a lawsuit, even for less serious injuries than may be required under your own provincial regulations. But don't get any ideas! Insurers are very serious about cracking down on insurance fraud, and that includes "staged" accidents.

29. Is automobile insurance different from one province to another?

Yes. Since auto insurance is provincially regulated, the rules change as you pass from one province to the next. The main difference lies in the accident benefits—the coverage that kicks in if you are injured or killed in a car accident—available through each province's insurance system; these may vary considerably from one province to another. However, your own insurance will cover you throughout the country.

In several provinces—Manitoba, British Columbia, Quebec, and Saskatchewan—compulsory, or basic, automobile insurance is handled solely by the government; private companies can sell only optional coverages in those provinces. Whether government-run or private, insurance systems change frequently, usually with the election of a new government. Therefore, we won't go into the details of each province's system, as that information would soon be outdated.

You won't be affected by the different provincial systems if you're travelling cross-country, unless you have an accident. If you are involved in an accident in another province, the rules of law where the accident took place would apply. So if you live in Ontario but have an accident in British Columbia, you would be subject to the regulations in British Columbia (even though you would still claim your accident benefits, if you were injured, from your own insurer). This could affect your claim significantly. For example, if you live in a province that allows lawsuits for injury, and you are injured in a province that has a pure no-fault system (meaning it compensates victims for bodily injury or death only by paying them no-fault accident benefits), you would not be permitted to sue the at-fault driver. The reverse situation, of course, could also apply.

Rather than studying the insurance systems of each province you pass through on your cross-country trip (even the experts have a tough time figuring them out), your best bet is to drive as safely as possible so you won't need to know at all.

30. If I live in a province that has "no-fault" insurance and I cause an accident, then it doesn't count as my fault, right?

Wrong! That's a common, and understandable, misconception on the part of consumers. The term "no fault" is misleading, to say the least. It really means that if you are injured or your car is damaged in an accident, you deal with your own insurance company, regardless of who was at fault. So if the other party was at fault, you don't have to go after that person's insurance company for compensation; your own company will pay for the loss or damage.

However, someone is still judged to be at fault, whether partly or completely. The law requires insurance companies to assign a percentage of fault for each of the drivers involved in the accident. This is done by using "fault determination rules" that are set out in a regulation under the Insurance Act. Fault determination rules are intended to help insurance companies deal with accident claims quickly and economically; consumers, however, may not always agree with the decision (see questions 31, 32, 33, and 34).

The percentage to which you are at fault will determine the amount of the deductible that you have to pay. For example, if you were found to be 50 per cent at fault, you would pay 50 per cent of the deductible on whatever coverage was paying for the repairs. Even if you were assigned only partial blame for the accident, your premium is likely to go up come renewal time.

If you were injured in the accident, you will still receive your accident benefit payments regardless of whether or not you were at fault. Your insurance company will pay benefits to you as the driver, as well as to anyone else injured in your vehicle who doesn't have his or her own automobile policy.

31. If I am not charged by the police in an accident, does that mean I am not at fault?

No. Insurance companies decide whether or not you are at fault based on regulations set out in the provincial Insurance Acts (see question 30). These "fault determination rules" are not related to charges laid or not laid by police under the Highway Traffic Act or the Criminal Code of Canada. This means that even though you may not have been charged by police for an accident, you can still be found at fault, either partially or completely, by the insurance company. By the same token, you could be charged by police, but determined to be not at fault for insurance purposes. If you are not at fault, your premiums should not go up; if, on the other hand, you are judged to be at fault to any degree, your premiums will increase.

SCENARIO

Taking A Hit In The Fender— And The Wallet

Q. You're driving along minding your own business. Another car sideswipes you, denting your fender, but doesn't stop.
Are you covered?
A. Only if you have Collision (or All Perils) insurance.
Otherwise, you're stuck with the repair bill, even though the accident wasn't your fault.

Fault determination rules cover more than 40 accident situations, using diagrams to illustrate specific accident scenarios. These rules are applied regardless of the circumstances of the accident—road or weather conditions, visibility, point of impact on the vehicles, or the actions of pedestrians, much to the chagrin of many consumers who believe there should be some leeway for poor conditions or other circumstances beyond their control (see question 32).

32. If a car is stopped in the middle of the road in a snowstorm and I rear-end it, am I considered to be at fault?

Yes. Even though the police may have told you that no one was at fault, according to rules set out in the Insurance Act for determining fault, you would be held at fault, since you hit the other car (see question 31). There is no allowance in the fault rules for extenuating circumstances. The way insurance companies see it, drivers are required to be in control of their vehicles at all times and to take road conditions into consideration. Case closed.

33. What if I disagree with the insurance company's assessment of fault?

Contact the person at the insurance company (not the brokerage) who handles consumer complaints. (In Ontario, every insurance company must have an ombudsperson; companies in other provinces may have someone in a similar capacity.) Ask that person what rule in the fault determination rules has been applied in your case (see questions 30 and 31). If you still disagree, you can submit your complaint in writing to the appropriate person at your provincial regulator (see "Consumer Resources" in Appendix A for contact information). However, the ombudsperson at the provincial regulator cannot determine fault in an accident, nor is the ombudsperson's decision binding on the insurance company. If you are still not satisfied, you may elect to go to court (see "Who ya gonna call?" in chapter 1 for a more detailed explanation). Less serious accidents can usually be dealt with in small claims court.

34. Does the insurance company ever change its decision about fault assessment?

Not usually. On occasion, an insurer may decide during the course of its investigation that it makes more sense to apply the law under the Highway Traffic Act or the Criminal Code, in other words, the law that would normally prevail if there were no fault determination rules. However, generally, it will probably change its decision only if new facts come to light; for example, if an eyewitness confirms that the other driver went through a red light as you were turning at an intersection. If this was the case and the company refused to consider this new information, you should lodge a complaint (see question 33).

35. What happens if I lend my car to my friend and he has an accident? Does his insurance cover it?

No! If you lend your car, you also lend your insurance. If your friend—or anyone else, for that matter, like a parking valet—has an at-fault accident while driving your car with your permission, it will go on *your* insurance record and you'll take the hit on your premium. Insurance does not follow the driver; it goes with the car.

However, there is a solution to this problem—the "27 endorsement," which covers damage to a car that you are driving but don't own (see ques-

SCENARIO

Lend Your Car, Lend Your Insurance

Q. You lend your car to a friend for the day, and she causes an accident. Does her own insurance cover it?

A. No. It goes on your insurance record, and your premium will likely increase as a result. If you lend your car, you also lend your insurance. So unless you're prepared to take the rap financially for someone else's at-fault accident, keep your car to yourself.

tion 25). This endorsement costs only about $25 to add to your automobile policy. It comes into play only if the policyholder is legally liable for the damage; otherwise, the other party's insurer pays.

The 27 endorsement can also be used for insuring rental cars, an economical alternative to purchasing the rental agency's collision damage waiver.

36. Why do young male drivers pay so much more for their insurance than other drivers? Is it legal for insurers to do this?

Unfortunately for single males under the age of 25, they are not an insurer's idea of a good risk. Statistics show that this group is much more accident-prone than others (see question 6). Therefore, these drivers represent a much higher risk to the insurance company, and are charged accordingly for their insurance. (Those who have passed an accredited driver education course, however, will generally pay considerably less, unless they have had an at-fault accident.)

Insurance rates are based on a number of risk factors, of which age, sex, and marital status are three (although sex and marital status are not relevant in rating older drivers). Young, single male drivers lose on all three counts. And yes, it is perfectly legal for insurers to rate drivers based on these risk factors. If young male drivers were charged less for their insurance, everyone else would have to pay more to subsidize them.

37. If my teenage son has taken driver training, do I have to submit any documentation to my insurance provider?

Yes, you need to submit his driver-training certificate before he can be considered for a premium discount.

38. If my son is driving my car, can he be insured as an occasional driver? How do insurance companies define "occasional driver?"

Yes, he can be insured as an occasional driver. The definition of an occasional driver will vary from one company to the next, but generally, insurers define "occasional driver" as someone under the age of 25 who drives the car not more than 50 per cent of the time (some companies may specify a lower percentage). You can likely get a further discount on the occasional driver's premium if your son or daughter is attending university or college as a full-time registered student and living more than 100 kilometres away from home (without the car, of course).

Note: If you have three cars and three drivers in your household, it is unlikely that insurance companies would agree to insure your son as an occasional driver since, in theory, he has access to a car at all times (see question 39).

39. My husband and I own three cars (we usually don't drive one of them in the winter). My son is only an occasional driver, but the insurance company wants to rate him as a full driver and charge a much higher premium, even though the cars are registered in my husband's and my name. Is this allowed?

Yes, it is allowed, and is common practice among insurers. And while it may seem like a money grab, there is some logic behind the practice. The thinking goes that, if there are three cars and three drivers, each driver must be rated as a principal driver. Since your son, in theory at least, has access to a car at all times, he cannot be rated as an occasional driver. Even though you may control your son's access to the car, if insurance companies did not take this position, sons and daughters everywhere would register their cars in the name of their parents and then claim to be occasional drivers. They'd save money on their insurance, but everyone else would have to pay more to subsidize their higher accident rate.

TIP

Bargains For Beginners

If you're a young and/or new driver, take a driver-training course from an approved school. It could save you as much as 40 per cent on your insurance in your first year of driving. Young drivers, especially males, take a real hit on their insurance premium, so this is one way to ease the pain.

However, if you are a long-term client with a good claims record, you may be able to convince your insurer to reconsider its position. It's worth a try.

40. My son has spent a lot of money renovating an old car. Can he put a specific value on it and insure it for that amount?

Yes, he can ask his insurance provider to add a "valued auto" endorsement (the terminology may differ from province to province) to his policy. This endorsement places a special value on the vehicle that has been agreed on by the policyholder and the insurance provider. If the car is damaged in an accident, the insurance company will pay up to the value indicated instead of "actual cash value" (the replacement value less depreciation). Your son would likely have to have an appraisal done to verify the higher value, and will be charged a higher premium.

If he has installed special permanent equipment, for example, a high-end stereo that is worth more than the amount covered under his Comprehensive insurance (usually $1,000), he can also purchase an endorsement to cover this.

41. If I buy a new car, is it automatically covered under my existing policy?

Your automobile policy provides automatic coverage for a newly acquired automobile, as long as your insurer is notified within 14 days of you taking delivery of the new car. However, for this coverage to apply, you must have all your vehicles insured with the same company. *Caution:* If one vehicle has less coverage than another—for example, if one doesn't have Collision insurance—then the coverage on the new vehicle would be the same as the *lowest* coverage on any existing vehicles. In this example, it would mean there would be no Collision insurance on the new car—obviously not a good idea.

The best solution is to arrange with your insurance provider for coverage on your new car *before* you pick it up. Use the automatic coverage only as a safety net if you are unable to reach your insurance provider before you take delivery of the car.

42. If something is stolen from my car, is it covered by my auto insurance?

No. Items stolen from your car that are not part of your car are covered under your homeowners or tenants policy. However, you would have to pay the deductible on that policy. Your claim would also be subject to the limits stated in your home policy (see chapter 2, questions 13, 27, and 28).

However, if the item that is stolen is part of the car—a stereo system, for example—it would be covered under the Comprehensive or All Perils (combination of Collision and Comprehensive) coverage on your auto policy, if you carry it (see questions 19 and 40). Again, the deductible would apply.

Therefore, if your car stereo and leather jacket are stolen from your car at the same time, you would have to pay the deductible on both your home policy and your auto Comprehensive policy, assuming you carry both coverages and want to claim for both items. (If both your home and auto insurance are with the same company, many insurers would charge you only the higher of the two deductibles.) Depending on what the deductible is on your home policy, it might not make sense to claim for that $400 jacket; perhaps your deductible is higher than the value of the jacket. Better lock it in the trunk instead.

43. If I stop driving for a number of years and then start again, will I have to pay for my insurance as if I were a new driver?

No, you shouldn't—and in some provinces you can't—be treated as a new driver. Although it was common in the past for insurance companies to penalize drivers who have a gap in their insurance coverage, this is no longer the case. (The exceptions would be if the lapse was due to cancellation of your policy for non-payment of premium, an accident that was not reported to the insurance company, or suspension of a driver's licence because of a conviction like impaired driving.) However, to be on the safe side, you should consider returning either to your previous insurance company or to a company with which you already have a history—like your property insurer—when you want to resume your coverage. Contrary to the old saying, familiarity *doesn't* breed contempt when it comes to insurance (unless, of course, you've been labelled a poor risk, in which case no company in the regular insurance market will want to touch you). You will need to prove you had prior insurance in order not to be rated as a new driver.

If you know there will be a lapse in your insurance, inform your insurance provider before you cancel your existing coverage, and ask for a letter outlining your policy number, insurance company, time insured, and claims history. It is also a good idea to prepare a letter in duplicate explaining why you are letting your coverage lapse. Have your insurance provider sign both copies, and leave one copy with him or her. That way, you will have proof of prior coverage when you need to reapply for insurance. If you have been driving outside the country, bring written proof of insurance from your previous country of residence.

44. Do I get a discount on my insurance if I'm over a certain age?

Yes, most companies offer discounts—usually in the range of 5 to 10 per cent—to drivers who are over 50 years old (the age limit may vary from 35 to 55) and who have a good driving record. Some insurance providers even specialize in insuring drivers of this age group; you may have seen the ads on television or heard them on the radio. If you fall into this category, ask your insurance provider what sort of discount is available to you. You may also get a price break for your years of claims-free Canadian driving experience; usually at least 20. Insurers in Ontario must offer a discount to retirees as well.

45. Can a Canadian student attending university in the U.S. and driving his or her own car keep a Canadian insurance policy?

As long as you still have a permanent residence in Canada and are just away to attend school, you can continue to use your Canadian insurance

TIP

When Older Is Better

If you're over 50, ask your insurance provider if you qualify for a mature driver discount on your car insurance.

policy. There is no time limit, and it is not necessary to obtain a driver's licence in the U.S. (see questions 27 and 28).

46. Can an insurance company increase the rates of an insured person based on the spouse's driving record, even if the spouse does not drive the insured person's vehicle?

They can, and they do. Insurers assume that even though the spouse does not normally drive the insured person's car, the opportunity is there for the spouse to do so.

There is an endorsement that can be added to your policy to exclude a specific driver, like your spouse, from using your vehicle. However, before you go to this extreme, consider the consequences. If your spouse had to drive your car in an emergency—even with your permission—and had an accident, the insurance would not pay for the damage.

47. If I shop around and find cheaper insurance, should I switch companies? If I do decide to change insurance providers, do I have to notify my current representative?

There are a couple of points to keep in mind as you decide. First, if you switch before your renewal date, you will likely be charged a penalty. The more months remaining on your policy, the higher the penalty.

Second, it is not a good idea to switch automobile insurers too often, or you can't build up a claims history with one company. With insurance companies, to know you is to like you (unless they think you've given them reason not to). For example, if you have built up a relatively good history with your current company and you have an at-fault accident, that company would be much more likely to "forgive" that accident and not increase your premiums than would a new company that isn't familiar with your record.

And even if you don't have a good history with your current company, you are unlikely to find a new company that will: a) agree to insure you at all; and b) charge you less than your existing company does. But if you can find such a beast, go for it! *Caution:* A company that charges *substantially* less than its competitors may not be your best ally come claims time. These companies keep their prices down by taking a hard line with claims.

Ask the new company what its policy is on at-fault accidents and mov-

Price Isn't Everything

Beware those insurance companies that charge substantially less than their competitors. They may tend to take a tougher stance at claims time, when you really need to count on your insurer.

ing violations, like speeding tickets. After all, you'd be worse off if you switched companies to save money on your premium, only to have an at-fault accident or speeding ticket that would drive up your premium even higher than what you were paying at your previous company, which is a distinct possibility.

Another consideration: If you have a speeding ticket or other moving violation on your Motor Vehicle Record (MVR), your current company may not discover it, unless it has a reason to run a check on your history. A new company, on the other hand, would likely check your driving record before agreeing to insure you. Alas, the ticket(s) would come to light, and your premium would be jacked up accordingly.

If you still decide to change companies, you are certainly free to do so, but you must notify your current insurance provider in writing. Don't think you can simply refuse to pay the renewal bill, or your account will be considered delinquent (see question 24).

48. If I have my brakes completely redone on my car for safety reasons, will my insurance pay for it?

No. It's your responsibility to maintain your car and ensure that it is safe to drive. No insurance will pay for wear and tear or gradual deterioration.

49. Does motorcycle insurance work the same way as car insurance?

Yes. Like car insurance, you can purchase motorcycle insurance from a broker, agent, group insurance plan (such as through a motorcycle association), or direct-response insurer. The cost of your insurance will be affected

The Switching Hour

If you plan to switch insurance companies, wait until your renewal date to do so, or you'll likely have to pay a penalty. And be sure to notify your previous insurer in writing. Simply ignoring the renewal notice won't send the right message—that's considered non-payment of premium and goes on your insurance record as a big black mark.

by the kind, size (generally, the bigger your motorcycle, the higher your premium), and age of your motorcycle, as well as your driving experience.

The same mandatory and optional coverages apply as for cars (see questions 4 and 5).

You may be able to save on your premium if you have completed a motorcycle riding course and if you have at least one year of riding experience.

The Claims Scenario

50. What should I do if I am involved in a fender-bender?

As long as no one was hurt, the first step is to exchange information with the other driver: name, address, driver's licence number, licence plate number, insurance policy number, and the name of the driver's insurance company. If the driver is not the registered owner of the vehicle, be sure to get that person's name and address too, as well as the names, addresses, and phone numbers of any witnesses. If you live in a city that has collision-reporting centres, as in parts of Ontario, for example, and if police were not at the accident scene, you must report to one of the centres with your vehicle within 24 hours; otherwise, notify the police. Police must be informed if there is $1,000 or more damage to any of the vehicles involved in the accident—and it doesn't take much to add up! Therefore, the safest policy is to notify the police.

However, if your accident took place on private property, for example, in a shopping centre, police will not come to the scene of the accident. Nonetheless, you still need to report it to them.

Once you have notified the police, you must report the accident to your insurance company within seven days, as stipulated in your policy. This applies whether you have damaged someone else's car or someone has damaged your car. Do not remove evidence of damage or repair the car until the company has had a chance to inspect your vehicle.

If you are the victim of a hit-and-run accident, many insurance companies will pay for the damage under your Collision insurance. Although you will have to pay the deductible, the accident will not affect your insurance record or premiums. If you don't carry Collision insurance, however, you're out of luck (see question 13).

If you were injured in the accident, your company will provide you with accident benefits claims forms that you must fill out before you can receive any benefits.

51. Should I make a claim if I am at fault in an accident and have sustained only minor damage to my car?

As long as you have not damaged someone else's car or injured anyone, and the damage to your car is not more than $1,000 (otherwise, you are obliged to report it to the police and your insurance company—see question 50), you are probably better off not to claim for the accident. That way, it will not go on your record, and your premiums will not increase as a result. Besides, you would have to pay the deductible on your Collision coverage anyway, so you probably wouldn't be out of pocket for much more if you paid for the repairs yourself. You'll save more in the long run by keeping your insurance record unblemished so your premiums don't increase.

Moreover, if you have too many at-fault claims in a short period of time, you risk having your policy non-renewed. Then you would have to shop around for a new insurer and likely pay an exorbitant price for coverage. Remember, it's not the amount paid out by the insurance company in a claim that counts against you; it's the question of fault. Therefore, an at-fault claim of only a few hundred dollars will count against your insurance record the same as a catastrophic at-fault accident would. Insurance is

Where Did That Tree Come From?
(And Other Likely Stories)

The following are actual statements found on insurance claim forms in which drivers attempted to summarize the details of an accident in the fewest possible words.

- I started to slow down, but the traffic was more stationary than I thought.
- Coming home, I drove into the wrong house and collided with a tree I don't have.
- The guy was all over the road. I had to swerve a number of times before I hit him.
- I was on the way to the doctor with rear-end trouble when my universal joint gave way, causing me to have an accident.
- My car was legally parked as it backed into another vehicle.
- I thought my window was down, but I found it was up when I put my head through it.
- I pulled away from the side of the road, glanced at my mother-in-law and headed over the embankment.
- I was thrown from my car as it left the road. I was later found in a ditch by some stray cows.
- To avoid hitting the bumper of the car in front, I struck a pedestrian.
- I knew the dog was possessive about the car but I would not have asked her to drive it if I had thought there was any risk.
- No witnesses would admit to having seen the mishap until after it happened.
- I didn't think the speed limit applied after midnight.
- I had been driving for 40 years when I fell asleep at the wheel and had an accident.
- The car in front hit the pedestrian but he got up so I hit him again.

there to cover the big losses that you couldn't afford otherwise, so pay for the minor repairs yourself and keep your insurance for when you really need it.

52. If I am at fault in a minor accident and inquire about making a possible claim to my agent or broker, will they report it to the insurance company, even if I decide not to make the claim?

If you deal through an independent broker, the broker would likely not report the accident to the insurance company if you decided not to make a claim. If, however, you are insured with a direct writer (which employs its own agents) or a direct-response insurer (which uses its own employees to insure you via telephone), the representative may be obligated by his or her employer to report it on your record. Consider inquiring anonymously if you are not sure whether or not you want to make a claim. (Remember, you *must* report it if there is more than $1,000 damage to your car or the other car(s)—see question 50.)

53. What happens if I get hit by a car that isn't insured, or by a hit-and-run driver?

If your car is damaged by a hit-and-run driver who cannot be identified, you must claim for the damage under your Collision or All Perils coverage. If you do not carry this insurance, you will have to pay for any repairs yourself.

In the case of an uninsured (but identified) driver, your Uninsured Automobile coverage, which is included with your basic automobile insurance (see question 4), will kick in. However, it is subject to a mandatory deductible that applies even if you aren't at fault in the accident.

54. How does the insurance company figure out how much to pay me if my car is totalled? What if I disagree with the amount it is offering?

As long as coverage is in place to repair or replace your car (Collision or All Perils), you will receive "actual cash value" for it. That means the replacement cost of your car *less* depreciation. If you were at fault in the accident, the insurer will subtract the deductible—either all or part of it, depending on whether you were completely or partially at fault—from that amount. The insurance company consults a used car valuation book (there are several different ones) or other market surveys to estimate the value of your vehicle.

If you disagree with the amount the insurer is offering to pay, do your own market research first. Consult publications like *Auto Trader* or *Automobile Red Book* to establish the realistic value of your car. Check with local car dealers, and read classified ads. Remember, the actual value does not mean the asking price on a used car lot, but the amount for which your car would realistically sell the day before the accident. High mileage and poor body condition, for example, would lower the value of a vehicle, while a rebuilt motor or transmission, recent paint job, or special equipment may increase it. If your car is in good condition, supply records of maintenance checks, along with any other work that has been done, like rustproofing, that could contribute to the proof of value. Sometimes it's hard to be objective when you have to replace your car with only the cash for its depreciated value in hand—especially if you weren't even at fault in the accident—but if insurers were to pay replacement value for every car that is damaged beyond repair, none of us would be able to afford the premiums the insurers would have to charge. *Note:* There is a special endorsement you can have added to your policy that limits depreciation charges under certain conditions (see question 56).

If you've done your research and still disagree with the amount being offered, you should discuss it with the claims manager and/or the insurance company ombudsperson (or the person appointed to deal with customer complaints). Ask how the amount was determined, and advise him or her of the research you have done. (You likely won't get far complaining about the amount if you have no figures to back you up.) If negotiations are unsuccessful, some provinces give you the right of appraisal, as outlined in the Insurance Act. However, you must pay the appraiser's fee, and the decision of the appraisal panel is final. If all else fails, your only recourse is legal action, either in small claims or a higher court, depending on the amount of money involved. You may also want to seek advice from the information officers at the Insurance Bureau of Canada's consumer information centre (see "Consumer Resources" in Appendix A for contact information).

Once you have accepted the insurer's offer for settlement, the salvage (what's left of your car) becomes the property of the insurance company. The company usually sells the salvage to a wrecker for parts.

Claim Form Questions

Q. Could either driver have done anything to avoid the accident?
A. Travelled by bus?
Q. What warning was given by you?
A. Horn
Q. What warning was given by the other party?
A. Moo

55. If the insurance company wants to give me a cash settlement for my car instead of repairing it, do I have to accept the offer, or can I get it repaired instead?

It is the insurance company's right to decide whether to repair the car or offer you a cash settlement instead. Even though you might think the car is repairable, the insurer may choose not to do so if it thinks this is not the most economical solution, or if it believes that the car might be unsafe to drive even after it has been repaired.

If you are determined to have your car repaired, you might be able to negotiate with someone in authority, like the claims manager (not the adjuster), but don't count on it. If the insurer refuses to repair the car, you are under no obligation to relinquish the salvage to the company, despite what the adjuster may tell you. But if you do not, you will not be able to receive a cash settlement, nor can you force the insurer to pay to repair your car. Your only option at that point would be to take the insurance company to court to force it to pay for the repairs.

56. My neighbour totalled her car and she got full value for it from the insurance company. Yet, when the same thing happened to my car, I got only the depreciated value for it. Why?

Your neighbour got full value for her car because she purchased a special endorsement that limits depreciation charges. This endorsement has several names—"limited depreciation policy," "removing depreciation deduction," "waiver of depreciation"—depending on the province in which you live. It says the insurance company will not charge depreciation within a specified time period (usually 24 to 36 months, depending on the province) if your car is damaged beyond repair in an accident.

In this case, the insurer will pay the lowest of the following amounts (less the deductible on your policy): the actual purchase price of the automobile and its equipment; the manufacturer's suggested list price on the car and its equipment on the original date of purchase; or the cost of replacing the automobile with a new one of the same make and model, similarly equipped. The payment includes all applicable taxes, but not tires, batteries, or paint.

You can request this endorsement when you are insuring a new car that you have just bought from a dealer. Just ask your insurance provider to add it on to your policy. At only about $25 a year, it's a real bargain. Without this feature, you would receive only actual cash value (replacement cost less depreciation) for your car if it were totalled in an accident. The difference could mean thousands of dollars. Unfortunately, insurance providers do not seem to widely promote it, so you likely have to ask. Nor do all insurers offer it. If yours doesn't, you might want to find one that does.

Note: For this endorsement to kick in, your car must be deemed a total loss by the insurer. No fender-benders!

TIP

No Sign Of Depreciation

If you're buying a new car, ask your insurance provider about getting an endorsement on your policy that limits depreciation charges if your vehicle is totalled within a specified period of time. While no one wants that to happen, you'll sure be glad you had the endorsement if it does!

57. If I am not at fault in an accident, do I still have to pay the deductible?

That depends. If the person who hit your car cannot be identified (as in a hit-and-run), your Collision insurance would have to pay for the damage, and you would have to pay the deductible on that coverage. If the other party is identified but not insured (even though it's illegal to drive without insurance, some people still do it), your "Uninsured Automobile" coverage would kick in, but again, you would have to pay a deductible (this amount may vary according to the regulations in your province).

If, on the other hand, the person who hit you is identified, insured, and totally at fault, his or her insurance will pay for the repairs and you will not have to pay a deductible. However, this may involve a waiting game in some provinces while the two insurance companies establish fault. Meanwhile, your car still needs to be repaired. Therefore, you may prefer to have your claim processed under Collision or All Perils insurance (if you carry this coverage), so you can get the repairs under way. In that case, you would pay the deductible and would be reimbursed once the other party's fault had been established. If you are found to be partially at fault, you will get back only a portion of your deductible. For example, if the deductible on your Collision insurance is $500 and you are found to be 25 per cent at fault, you will be reimbursed $375, rather than the full $500.

58. Do I have a choice where I take my car to be repaired? Do I have to get more than one estimate?

You have the right to go to the repair shop of your choice, as long as the insurer approves the estimate. Most insurance companies work with body shops that they have certified and approved—known as "preferred providers"—and which will guarantee the repairs. Some consumers may find using these easier, because it not only eliminates the "competitive quotes" process, but also puts the onus on the insurer to make sure the work is done satisfactorily.

If you prefer to find a repair shop yourself, you are not necessarily required to get more than one estimate, but neither is the insurance company obliged to accept the price that you want it to pay for repairs. It is not likely to pay any higher cost than the price quoted by its recommended repair shop. Therefore, getting more than one estimate is one way of establishing a price that is fair to both parties. If the insurance company will not meet the price quoted by the repair shop of your choice, try to resolve the problem with your insurer's claims manager.

59. Does the insurance company have the right to replace parts in my car with used parts when it is being repaired after an accident?

The insurance policy says that the company has the right to repair, rebuild, or replace any damaged parts with other parts "of like kind and quality." That means that if you rear-end a car and damage the bumper on your four-year-old car, the insurer will likely replace your bumper with a used one of the same kind and quality as the original. If insurers were to replace old parts with new, our insurance premiums would be a lot higher (see question 60).

Unlike your homeowners policy, which is usually sold on the basis of replacement cost (meaning that lost or damaged items are replaced at today's value), automobile repairs are made on an actual cash value basis. That means that depreciation is taken into account when your car is repaired. The bottom line: no new parts for older ones.

If it is a safety-related issue, it's a different story. For example, a worn tire would be replaced with a new one. However, in that case, you are expected to pay the difference between the new tire and the actual cash value of your existing tire (see question 60).

60. If my car door is replaced following an accident, but the paint doesn't exactly match the other doors, shouldn't my insurance pay for repainting the whole car?

It's understandable that consumers would expect insurers to do this. It's bad enough having to suffer the inconvenience of doing without your car for several days, especially if you didn't even cause the accident, and naturally, you want your door to match the rest of the car, as it did before. However, your insurance won't pay to have your whole car repainted if only one door was damaged. Otherwise, you'd end up better off than you were before the accident, with a new paint job on an older car. This is known as "betterment."

You can insist on having your whole car repainted, but you will have to make up the difference in cost, or agree with the insurer on the amount of your contribution to the new paint job. Different companies have different policies in this regard, and often a decision is made on a case-by-case basis. Discuss it with your insurer and negotiate your contribution.

Insurance is intended to put things back to the way they were before, not to make them better than they were. If insurance companies were to pay for repainting an entire car to repair a scratch in one door, we would all pay higher premiums. It's up to insurance providers to explain this to consumers, and many of them fail to do so.

Checklist

Top 10 questions to ask your insurance provider before you buy or renew your automobile insurance

1. What—and who—does my policy include?
2. How can I save money on my automobile insurance without compromising my coverage?
3. Do I qualify for any discounts?
4. What optional coverages are available?
5. Should I carry both Comprehensive and Collision coverage?
6. How much liability coverage do I have? Should I increase it?
7. What is my deductible? What do you recommend?
8. Does the insurance company forgive one at-fault accident? If not, by how much will my premium go up?
9. How will a moving violation affect my rating (and premium)?
10. Is there 24-hour claims service? What is the claims procedure? Does the company provide any emergency support services, like towing?

Keywords

All Perils coverage	optional insurance that combines Collision and Comprehensive insurance. Subject to a deductible.
At-fault accident	an accident in which you are considered to be at fault, either completely or partially, and which will go on your insurance record;

this is regardless of whether or not you have been charged by police. Therefore, you can still be considered at fault by your insurance company, even if you are not charged under the Highway Traffic Act.

Collision or Upset insurance
optional insurance that pays to have your car repaired or replaced when it is involved in a collision, whether with another car, a telephone post, or any other object (but not with animals). Subject to a deductible.

Comprehensive insurance
optional insurance that pays to replace loss or damage to your car *other than* that caused by Collision or Upset, including damage caused by falling or flying objects, missiles, explosion, flood, earthquake, fire, theft, vandalism, and collision with animals. Therefore, it is broader than Specified Perils coverage (see below). Subject to a deductible, except in cases of theft and fire.

Deductible
the portion of a claim that you agree to pay. This applies to mandatory Uninsured Automobile coverage, as well as optional coverages like Collision, Comprehensive, and All Perils. It does not apply to theft (of the whole vehicle), fire, or lightning claims. Most insurance companies have a minimum acceptable deductible, but you can choose a higher one in order to save money on your premium.

Facility Association
an industry-sponsored insurance pool "of last resort" for high-risk drivers—those with several "at-fault" claims and/or driving convictions—when insurance can't be placed with a regular company. Rates are much higher—possibly as much as 250 per cent more, depending on the offence. All car insurance companies belong to Facility Association. (Provinces with government-run automobile insurance systems do not belong to it, but still surcharge high-risk drivers.)

No-fault insurance
insurance system whereby accident victims collect benefits, up to a specified amount, for certain medical expenses and lost income from their own insurance companies, regardless of who was at fault. Lawsuits are allowed only in cases of severe injury.

Specified Perils
optional insurance against loss or damage caused by specific perils, or causes of loss. These usually include: fire, theft, lightning, windstorm, hail, earthquake, explosion, falling aircraft or parts of aircraft; or the destruction of any kind of vehicle in which the insured automobile is being transported. However, it does not normally include vandalism, or rock chip damage to windshields. Subject to a deductible.

life insurance

Three main reasons to buy life insurance

The difference between term, term to 100, and permanent life policies

How much coverage you need

How to choose an agent or broker

What happens when you apply for life insurance

Life Insurance: Who Needs It?

WHOEVER NAMED IT "LIFE" INSURANCE had a magnificent way with words. Why? Because "life" insurance really isn't about life at all; it's mostly about death—your death and what your beneficiaries are entitled to after you've drawn your last breath (assuming, of course, you were astute enough to have a life policy in the first place). Transforming death into life was a pretty sharp move on the part of insurance companies. It's a whole lot more saleable than the alternative.

Buying a life policy could be the smartest purchase you ever make. And because it may cost you more over the long run than that new Jeep Cherokee you have your eye on, it's a good idea to know exactly what you're purchasing, what kind of coverage you're getting, and whether you're getting fair value. Which means paying attention to some basics.

There are many different types of life insurance on the market. Some types of policies will suit your needs and your bank account. Many others will not. The only way you will know which to choose is to spend at least as much time researching this purchase as you would any other major purchase. Then you'll know what questions to ask your insurance agent or broker, and what answers to expect.

This chapter does not address group insurance, or the finer points of how to use life insurance as an instrument for savings and investing. Just some basics about a very complex subject.

Life insurance is not for everyone. Most single people and many couples without children will probably not need a life policy, but this doesn't always stop life insurance salespeople from trying to sell them something anyway. The rule of thumb is, unless you have dependents who rely on the

Insurance Humour, Circa 1914

"Madam, can I sell your husband some life insurance?"
"I don't think so. I'm afraid he's not long for this world."
"Then how about some fire insurance?"
—Canadian Insurance *magazine, 1914*

financial support you have regularly provided up until your untimely death, you don't need life insurance. You may choose to have a life policy if your spouse is not earning an income and doesn't wish to re-enter the workforce after your death, but that's not the same as having a bereaved wife or husband and three small children wondering where the next car payment and groceries are coming from. Other reasons for buying life policies include covering a business partner, or paying taxes on property investments so your spouse won't see your return dwindle substantially after your death.

These days, there is much more disclosure about life insurance policies than there was 10 or 20 years ago. Until recently, some policies, particularly those in the category of permanent insurance (that is, "whole" and "universal" life) were a licence to print money—for the insurance companies, that is. Some still are, so ask for numerous competitive quotes. Don't be afraid to ask all the questions you can think of during the early stages of your quest for life insurance. This can be an eye-opening experience. (Remember the old adage: There are no stupid questions, just stupid answers.)

Three types of policies

There are essentially three types of life insurance policies:

1. Term insurance: This is bare-bones life insurance, which allows you to purchase a death benefit that suits your needs, and renew or change it at the end of the specified term, say, 10 or 20 years.
2. Permanent insurance, including "whole" and "universal" life: These include an investment component, as well as a "cash value" option

which allows you, after several years, to cash in the policy (at the same time giving up the death benefit). It may be paid off prior to death.

3. Term to 100 insurance: essentially, permanent term insurance.

For more about these types of insurance, see page 127.

Once you've purchased a life policy, there's a tendency to say "that's that" and never think about it again. You would be wise, however, to review your coverage periodically, since many things that were of initial concern change over time—your kids grow up and get jobs (you hope!), your mortgage is paid off, you win the lottery and the family doesn't need the same financial support...

Sir Wilfrid Laurier on Life Insurance

"When I was young, I was in very delicate health. Thank the Lord, I have good health now. I was 30 before I could get an insurance on my life. I had applied to a company and they had refused me. I don't blame them for it. They refused till in 1878, when I was 36, the Sun Life consented to take the risk. They did so on the advice of Mr., now Sir, James Grant, who said I was good for 10 years only (laughter). But

when once the ice was broken, then it was easy to get insured in any other company. The Sun would not take me on the whole life, but only on the 10-year plan. It still exists, and I have to die to get the money.

But as evidence of how little I regard money, I have, in all these years, never fulfilled that requirement which would compel the company to pay."

(Canadian Insurance magazine's August 27, 1913, coverage of Sir Wilfrid Laurier's speech at the Life Underwriters' convention that year in Ottawa; Laurier had been Prime Minister until 1911.)

Author's note: Not many people nowadays get turned down for life insurance— only about 3 per cent. And 94 per cent receive the coverage they apply for at standard (regular) rates.

There's a big difference between life insurance and other types of insurance. Property coverage for your home, car, and business is renewed annually, and you will never collect a cent; that is, you'll never collect if you're lucky enough not to experience any of the misfortunes that trigger a claim. With life insurance, there is always a payoff at the end (unless you let your coverage lapse). But, given that death activates the claim, most people would prefer to keep right on paying the premium. Here's to your long and healthy life!

Frequently Asked Questions ...
About Life Insurance

1. Why do I need life insurance?

There are a number of reasons for buying life insurance. First and foremost, you will likely buy life insurance to protect your family or those who depend on you for financial support. You buy life insurance to replace the income that would be lost if you die before your estate has grown sufficiently to look after your family's, or other dependents', needs. It's really insuring your future income.

Second, you will likely buy life insurance when you purchase a home and take out a mortgage. The bank or financial institution holding your mortgage will want to protect its investment—that gigantic loan to you—and the easiest way is with a policy on your life, enough to pay off the balance of the mortgage if you die before it is paid off. This makes a lot of sense. In the event of your untimely death, your spouse, children, and any other dependents will continue to have a roof over their heads, mortgage-free, as well as money to pay for your funeral.

Third, if you run a business with a partner, you may want to consider taking a life insurance policy in his or her name. If he or she dies suddenly, the money from the life insurance policy would allow you to buy the other half of the business from your partner's estate and carry on.

Finally, there are also certain tax advantages. For example, the person whom you name as beneficiary on your life policy will not have to pay estate

The Gift That Keeps On Giving

*Consider leaving money to charity by taking out a life insurance
policy and naming your favorite organization as beneficiary. If
the charity is registered, the premiums will be tax-deductible.*

taxes if you die. Some types of plans (Universal Life) allow you to keep a
portion of your payments in a tax-sheltered reserve fund (see page 132).

2. When do I buy life insurance?

The short answer is you buy life insurance when you need it. You wouldn't
consider buying auto insurance if you don't own a car. Similarly, if you're
living alone with no dependents, no house, no mortgage, no business to
protect, then you don't need life insurance.

But if you do have dependents—a partner not working or with insuffi-
cient income to carry the full financial load, children still at home or
attending college, aging relatives—that is, anyone who counts on your support—then you need life insurance. And if you don't already have coverage, don't wait much longer before getting some.

Ironically, people often need life insurance when they themselves have
the least money and the heaviest financial responsibilities: young children,
a new house (and mortgage), a start-up business, or an entry-level salary. In
theory, the number of people who depend on you should decline as you get
older, but this is not always the case, especially these days. Since more people are living longer and job security seems to be a thing of the 1950s and
1960s, you may end up supporting your parents, adult children, and even
your grandchildren for a while.

3. Whom do I insure?

You want to insure the people who support your household through their
salary, their work in the home, or both. For example, if you are the one who

goes out to work or, equally likely today, downstairs to your home office, you may consider taking out a life insurance policy. The policy should provide enough income to your dependents for as long as they need it.

You should also consider taking out a policy on your spouse or partner if that person works at home taking care of children, aging relatives, and the house. This life insurance policy should provide enough income to cover the costs you will likely incur if your partner died. These may add up to a considerable sum: housekeeping, babysitting, daycare, and after-school care for the kids—even special care for elderly relatives.

Make sure that both policies cover the cost of paying off any outstanding debts, especially the mortgage, but more on this later.

You probably don't need to insure your children unless they operate a major paper route and pay part of the mortgage with their earnings. As a rule, children don't contribute substantially to the income of the household, so they don't need to be insured. However, there are policies today that can provide a child with funds for higher education, while covering both the child and parent. So it is your personal choice, and you may choose to have policies for your children.

4. Who benefits from my death?

Whom you name as your beneficiary is up to you. But there are two main points to keep in mind while making your decision. First, life insurance death benefits are tax-free and creditor-proof, as long as the named beneficiary is not your estate. Your estate is responsible for paying all your debts after you die. If you name it as your beneficiary, then all your creditors, including Revenue Canada, stand in line ahead of your partner and family.

CAUTION

A Taxing Situation

If you name your estate as the beneficiary of your life insurance policy, probate fees and taxes will likely apply.

Protect Support Payments

If you're divorcing, make sure your support payments are life-insured. You can do this in two ways: make it part of the divorce agreement that your ex-partner takes out a life policy to cover support payments and names you as beneficiary; or (with your ex's approval) take out a life policy yourself in your ex-spouse's name, making yourself the beneficiary. You pay the premiums, but you're also in control and no one can cancel the policy.

If, however, you make your spouse or partner the beneficiary, she or he is entitled to all the benefits. While your dependents may choose to clear the slate and pay your debts after your death, that choice evaporates if you name your estate as beneficiary. Also be aware that, if you name a business partner or company as beneficiary, the benefits are not creditor-proof.

The second consideration is that the first person you name as beneficiary may predecease you or die at the same time, as in the case of an auto accident. Hence, you will probably want to consider naming a contingent beneficiary, such as your children (or any others you support).

You can also name the beneficiary as irrevocable. This means that if you decide to change the beneficiary at a later date, you must have the permission of the current beneficiary.

5. How much insurance do I need to buy?

There is a short and long answer to this question.

First, the short answer: You want to buy a policy with death benefits that will cover the immediate and long-term financial needs of the people who depend on you. So, the rule of thumb is to multiply your gross income (income before taxes) five to seven times. This is roughly how much insurance you need to buy. So, with a gross income of $50,000, you should be looking for coverage in the $250,000 to $350,000 range.

Now the long answer: Add up all your immediate and long-term monthly expenses. Total your income from investments and other insurance benefits; subtract this from the long-term expenses. The difference is the amount your death benefit must cover each month. These expenses typically include:

- Immediate expenses—These may include funeral costs, taxes, probate fees, costs incurred because of your illness or accident, and enough money to cover a period of adjustment after your death. These are not cheap items as a rule.

- Funeral expenses—The average cost of a modest funeral, cemetery plot, and headstone runs between $6,000 and $10,000. This does not include flowers, costs associated with the wake afterwards, or other extras.

- Expenses from your illness or accident—These may include private-duty nursing, special medication, and perhaps hospital expenses, if the accident occurred outside Canada and is not covered by travel insurance.

- Period of adjustment—This money may help to cover extraordinary expenses incurred by your beneficiary during the six months to a year after your death. These expenses may include grief counselling, moving the household, and learning (or re-learning) job skills.

- Estate taxes—When you die, Revenue Canada values your assets (such as your cottage and home) at the date of death, then taxes the estate accordingly. If you have an estate of some size, or assets that may be subject to capital gains, you may want to add a line here for an accountant's fee. Note: Any assets that are jointly owned, like your home, are not taxed, but rather transfer to the surviving spouse.

- Income tax—Further, the executor files an income tax form for the income earned that year. If your income taxes are deducted at source, there is no problem. But if you work for yourself and do not pay tax every quarter, or if you've deferred taxes, you'll want to add more money to pay income taxes.

- Probate fees—Each province charges a fee or a tax to cover the cost of "probating" the will—that is, registering it with the courts. The fee is usually a percentage of the estate's value. In Ontario, for instance, the tax proposed to replace the fee on estates worth more than $50,000 is $15 for every $1,000.

- Long-term expenses—These include your ongoing bills, as well as daycare fees, college or university tuition, entertainment and vacation, and a 10-percent contingency fund. (For more about these expenses, see below.)
- Current monthly expenses—These include rent, condo fees or mortgage (if you do not have mortgage insurance), as well as food, hydro, water, telephone, heat, and yes, even those Internet server bills.
- Other regular expenses—These include clothing, daycare, or after-school care, medical and dental expenses.

Other expenses

- University or college tuition—The annual tuition fees for an undergraduate university degree in Ontario in 1998–1999 averaged $5,000. That does not include the cost of books, residence, or food, which can add another $5,000 to $10,000 to the bill.
- Car care and insurance—Be sure to include the average annual cost of maintaining and insuring your car or cars.
- Entertainment and vacation—This is self-explanatory, but often forgotten. Your dependents will no doubt appreciate taking the kind of vacations to which you have all become accustomed.
- Contingency fund—You may want to add 10 per cent either as a contingency fund or to cover inflation, which in 1998 was running at about 1 per cent a year.
- Future monthly income—This includes the income your partner earns, as well as your investments, other insurance policies (such as those at work), and government pensions such as the Veteran's Pension.

By subtracting your monthly income from monthly expenses, you get the expected monthly shortfall in income that your death benefits need to cover.

TIP

How Much Is Enough?

How much life insurance do you need? A good rule of thumb is five to seven times your gross income.

Multiply this figure by 12, which gives you your annual shortfall; that is, how much interest income your death benefits need to generate every year to adequately support your partner, children, and elderly relatives. How long that is depends on many factors, including the age of the children and, if known, how long they may be in university (you're hoping, surely, that they don't all have eyes on PhDs).

At present, one- to five-year savings certificates with the country's major financial institutions earn 3 to 5 per cent interest annually. Whatever figure you use to work out how much insurance you need, do not overestimate the interest rates. They have hovered between 3 and 5 per cent for about five years.

6. What are the different types of insurance policies?

There are three main kinds of policies—term, permanent, and term to 100.

- Term insurance covers you for a specified length of time, usually 1, 5, 10, or 20 years.
- Permanent insurance, which includes whole life and universal insurance, covers you for your whole life.
- Term to 100 is essentially no-frills permanent insurance.

7. What are the features and advantages/disadvantages of each kind?

Term insurance

As its name suggests, term insurance covers you for a specific period of time—usually 1, 5, 10, or 20 years, or until you are 70 or 80 years old. Term insurance is not generally sold beyond age 80. Whatever the policy's length, insurance companies pay death benefits only if you die while it is in force. When the policy's term finishes, you may either renew the existing policy or buy a different type of life insurance policy, such as whole or universal life.

Premiums: With term policies, you pay the same premium each month for the length of the policy. However, the premiums may, and probably will, rise when and if you renew a term policy. That's because you're older and your chances of dying have increased. This risk is reflected in your insurance costs.

Questions to ask about term policies: Bare bones, you should ask at least the following three questions when you buy term insurance.

1. *Will the company issuing my policy guarantee renewal without a medical examination, even if I change careers (from sales clerk to stunt person) or develop a health problem?*

   As with nearly all other types of life coverage, the insurance company will probably require you to have a medical examination when you apply for term insurance. If you are twenty-something at the time you purchase your first policy, the medical examination will probably turn up nothing serious. If you buy a 10- or 20-year term policy, you will be 30 or even 40-plus when it expires. A checkup at that time may reveal problems.

   Most term policies in Canada allow you to renew your term insurance without taking another medical examination. This is a crucial feature for an aging policyholder, in part because most serious diseases, such as cancer and heart disease, will occur more frequently with age. Guaranteed renewal gives you peace of mind; you know you will be able to renew your policy no matter what your state of health. It's really the only way to go.

2. *Is it possible to convert my term policy into a whole life or universal life policy without a medical exam?*

   The issue of "convertibility" is likely very important to you, especially if your term insurance ends when you are 55 or 65 years old, and you want to purchase a policy you can keep for life.

3. *Does the company guarantee its renewal rate for the policy?*

   If you're not a gambler at heart, you may want to buy a term policy with a guaranteed—not negotiable—premium at renewal. While the price will be higher at renewal (you're older and less invincible), you will know from the contract what your financial obligation will be.

The pros and cons of term insurance: As with most things in life (pun actually intended), there are several advantages and one main disadvantage to buying a term policy.

There are three main benefits to term insurance:

• You can tailor a term insurance policy to fit your changing needs. To illustrate, say you have three young children when you buy your first policy. For at least 20 years, they will most likely be dependent on you, so you will want to protect them satisfactorily for this period of time. After they've flown the nest, however, your need for coverage drops significantly. A 20-year term (or combinations of shorter term with guaranteed renewal rates) fits your need to a T.

- When you're young, term insurance is less expensive to buy than whole life or universal life policies—in most cases, substantially less expensive. This makes it affordable when you have major financial responsibilities coupled with a lower income, and yet you need a lot of coverage.
- Finally, if you buy a renewable and convertible term insurance policy (do this even though it will cost you a little more!), you know you will be able to renew it or convert it to some form of permanent life insurance when the term is up.

There is one main disadvantage to term insurance:

- The premium increases every time you renew your policy (but, as noted above, only if you carry the same amount of coverage. If you choose to drop the face value of the policy significantly, the premium may also drop, even though you're older.)

Another consideration: Term insurance is not suitable for estate planning; there's no payout if you don't renew, or if you live past 80 and your policy terminates (which in itself is a big bonus!).

One last (but crucial) point: Many insurance agents/brokers will tell you that term insurance lacks the "cash value" or "dividend" features of permanent insurance policies (although some term policies do pay a dividend based on favourable portfolio mortality or expense results).

To explain: The premiums for a whole life policy are the same from the time you buy it until you have paid it off, or die.

When you are young and the risk of dying is lower, the company sets aside the difference between what you pay and the actual cost of insuring you—called the "mortality charge." The company uses the money to fund the policy later when you are older, the risk of your dying greater, and your mortality charge higher.

If you cash in the policy, the company will return some of the money that it has held in reserve all those years. This is the cash value of the policy. If you die, the insurance company pays the death benefit, but keeps the cash value.

Dividends are a variation on this theme. Some permanent insurance policies are what the companies call "participating." That is, the company gives back to you each year some of the money you have paid. This payment, which is not a guaranteed amount, is called a dividend. (In both cases, please note, the company is giving you back your own money.)

Permanent insurance

Whole life insurance

A whole life policy is designed to be kept for—yes—your whole life. Hence the name. If that is not your intention, then this policy may not be the one for you.

Insurance companies fix the premiums for the whole of the policy's life. You will probably pay the same premium when you make your first payment as you will towards the end of your life. Many companies will let you pay more for this coverage more quickly, in 5 to 15 years, for example, with much higher payments. As with an accelerated mortgage, this route is often less expensive in the long run.

However you pay for your whole life policy, part of your premium covers the actual cost of the insurance. This is called the "mortality charge." The mortality charge is computed by actuaries—the number crunchers—who base their calculations on many factors, such as:

- the rate of death among people in different age groups;
- health of the applicant;
- type of job the applicant holds (bean counter versus bungee jumper);
- risky habits (smoking, drinking, taking drugs);
- what the insurers consider to be hazardous hobbies (skydiving, car racing, scuba diving).

Not surprisingly, the mortality charge increases with age. In addition to the mortality charge, the company also deducts a sum to cover its administrative, management, and overhead costs. (This is true of all policies, not just permanent insurance.)

With whole life policies, part of the premium also goes into a "reserve" to help cover the cost of your steadily increasing mortality charge. The money

Change with the Times

Once you've bought a life insurance policy, you may think it's something you'll never have to think about again. But you should review your family and business situation regularly to make sure you're adequately covered. (And even though we're in a period of calm now, once inflation gets rolling, it can quickly eat away the value of your insurance.)

in reserve earns interest. Insurance companies, however, do not have to disclose how much interest the reserve is accruing.

Two features of whole life insurance:

1. Cash value—Insurance companies set aside part of this money in reserve and call it the "cash value" of the policy. All whole life policies build cash values that grow over the length of the policy. You receive the cash value if you give up your whole life insurance. (This may be a smart move, for example, when your financial responsibilities for dependents have dwindled, or your beneficiary dies before you do.) You can also access the cash value if you take out a policy loan.

   If you die before cancelling the policy, the insurance company pays out the death benefit but keeps the cash value. You have various options as to the payout. Unlike death benefits, cash values are taxable, so you may want to ask your agent or broker about an annuity instead of a lump sum payout.

   Although the insurance company controls the cash value of a whole life policy, you may borrow against it. If you do, the company sets the interest rate. If you die before you've paid off the loan, the company deducts the outstanding debt plus interest from your death benefit.

2. Dividends—Some whole life policies are called "participating" policies. They're called this because insurance companies say you participate in the financial life of the company.

If all goes well—for example, fewer people die than expected—companies pay you a dividend. However, unlike the dividends that a mining or petroleum company may pay stockholders from its profits, insurance company dividends come out of the premiums that you have already paid.

Two points to remember about participating policies:

1. The premiums will likely be higher than for "non-participating" policies.
2. The amount you receive as a dividend is not guaranteed. On the other hand, because these dividends come out of your premiums, they're not taxed.

You can take dividends as cash, use them to reduce your premiums, or leave them on deposit to accumulate interest which, like all interest, is taxable. Or you can use your dividends to buy extra amounts of insurance, sometimes called "paid-up additions." They're called "paid-up" because you buy these small extra policies outright and no more premiums are due; and "additions" because they are in addition to the policy you already have.

Universal life insurance

Universal life combines the term insurance policy with flexible premiums and a separate savings program which, to some extent, you direct. This is a hybrid policy that offers special benefits in particular to people who need tax shelters. Not for the faint-hearted, this policy is complex, comes in many forms, and requires a great deal of thought and attention. That said, if you buy a universal policy, the insurance company usually pays your beneficiary the death benefits *and* the money from the savings component or the cash value of the policy.

It offers two death benefit options: the fixed amount of insurance that you purchased; and the fixed amount plus the money that has accumulated in the savings component of the policy. The first choice is cheaper, but the second choice offers a greater gain to the beneficiary.

Universal life policy premiums are flexible to a point. They must cover the insurance company's administrative, management, and overhead costs, as well as pay the immediate and ever-growing future cost of insuring you. As with whole life insurance, part of your premium goes into a reserve to help cover the immediate and future cost of insuring you. The money in reserve earns interest and is generally not taxable.

When you buy universal life insurance, ask for quotes on the minimum, target, and guaranteed maximum premium charges:

- The minimum premium will pay all the immediate costs and put enough money into the reserve account to pay for your insurance.
- The target premium will do that and allow you to build up your reserve or the cash value of your policy.
- The guaranteed maximum expense and mortality charge is the most the company may charge you annually for the life of the policy. This is good to know because if the company's costs increase, it will pass them through to you in the charges it deducts from your fund. This will cause your policy to expire, unless you make additional payments. Ask for the "COI," which is the monthly mortality charge that the company assesses with respect to the universal life policy.

Universal versus whole life

Universal insurance differs from whole life insurance in several ways:

- First, with a universal life policy, you may, if you wish, change the death benefits. Decreasing the death benefit is routine; however, increasing it requires permission by the company. It may ask for further medical information and, based on that, may increase your fee.
- Second, with a universal life policy, you may choose to pay much more than the cost to cover your insurance. The difference between your actual costs and what you have paid stays in a tax-sheltered reserve fund to earn interest. Canada's income tax laws, however, do limit how much you may shelter in the reserve in the same way they limit your annual contributions to your registered retirement savings plan (RRSP).
- Third, with a universal life policy, you control the savings in the reserve account. This means that you may use the money from the reserve account to make a premium payment or two. But do so with caution, because you must keep enough money in this account to cover your ever-increasing mortality charge.
- Fourth, with a universal life policy, you decide how to invest the money in the reserve account. Most companies offer several choices, ranging from daily-interest savings accounts and guaranteed investment certificates to mutual funds and mortgages.

The pros and cons of permanent insurance

Permanent policies have several advantages over term insurance:

- They cover you for your whole life, which is a consideration in financially unstable times.
- Second, you can buy a policy with unvarying premiums. The premiums are fixed; they don't change one iota from the first year of the policy to the last (unless you choose to accelerate your payment).
- Other advantages include the cash value, which you can borrow against, and the possibility of receiving dividends.

There are three main disadvantages to permanent insurance:

- When you're just starting out and have many financial responsibilities, permanent insurance may cost too much to afford the protection you need.
- Permanent insurance is not a cost-effective way to cover your short-term needs.
- The cash values of whole life and universal policies tend to be very limited in the early years of the policy.

It is important to note that many companies charge a fee to universal policyholders who surrender their policies. This surrender charge may take a huge bite out of your savings in the reserve account. Be sure to ask what these surrender charges are.

CAUTION

If You Cash In, You Can't Cash Out

You may wish to cash in your permanent insurance policy at some point in the future. Remember that if you decide to take the cash value, you forfeit the death benefit. However, you don't have to surrender the policy to get at the cash—you can use the policy loan feature.

Term to 100

A term to 100 policy insures the holder until age 100—or for life. The difference between it and whole life insurance is that this policy has no cash value and does not pay dividends—usually. (With insurance there are always exceptions, so ask!)

Like a regular term policy, term to 100 premiums are set for the life of the policy, but because it covers the whole of your life (unless you live to 105), the premiums are higher than regular term insurance, at least at first.

8. How do I know if the policy is good value?

It is difficult to figure out what is good value when you're knee deep in insurance company promotional material, each insurer touting the value of its own products, and each plan sporting such a wide variety of bells and whistles that one is never exactly comparable to another.

At this point, remember why you set out to buy life insurance: To protect the financial well-being of your dependents? Or to create a savings plan or a tax shelter? You may also want to look again at how much you need to buy, how long you want to be covered, and how much insurance you can afford to pay. If you find a policy that fits your needs, it is probably good value.

Remember, you're buying a life insurance policy to provide peace of mind to your partner, children, and perhaps to elderly relatives, not to the insurance salesperson (who, by the way, earns a much heftier commission on whole life and universal life policies than on term insurance).

If term insurance fits your needs and your budget now, ask the insurance salesperson to provide you with the facts on at least 5 to 10 different policies that have the death benefits you need at a price you can afford. Of course, you should be able to convert any policy you might buy into a permanent policy, and to renew it without taking a medical examination. These policies should also have guaranteed renewal rates.

To figure out which policy is the best value, add up the premium rates for the number of years you need insurance—10, 20, or 30 years, for example. The policy that offers the cheapest rates for the first 5 or 10 years may end up being the most expensive of the bunch when you add in the cost of the premiums for the next 2-, 5-, or 10-year periods.

If whole life insurance gives you peace of mind, you may want to compare prices by adding the cost of the premiums from now until you reach 75 or 85 years old. That is the cost of the policy. Ignore the cash value. When you die, your beneficiary or beneficiaries receive the death benefits, but not the cash value. The insurance company keeps that.

Comparing the costs of universal life insurance policies is difficult because the premiums you pay, interest rates on your investment account, and sometimes even the death benefits can fluctuate. For peace of mind, ask all the questions you can think of, including:

- Are there guaranteed minimum and maximum premium charges? If so, what are they?
- What interest rate is the insurance company using to illustrate this proposed policy of mine? (Less scrupulous life insurance companies have been known to cite rates from the early 1980s, back in the good old days when interest was up over 20 per cent. Makes just about any policy look very tempting.)
- What mortality rates is the company using?
- How much are the management or administration fees the company charges?
- Are there participating dividends? (These allow you to buy more units and increase the cash value of your policy.)
- Can I borrow money from the policy at a rate that is lower than the market?

9. What are "illustrations"? And how can they guide— or misguide—me?

In theory, an "illustration" presented by a life insurance provider is designed to answer your questions about the cost and value of the specific policy you are considering. In practice, life insurance illustrations can confuse all but the most accomplished in the field of insurance. Sad to say, some of this confusion is calculated, because some life agents are less than scrupulous (an unfortunate fact of life in any profession).

About 10 years ago, the British government passed a law that specified what information life insurance illustrations must include. The U.S. has instituted similar guidelines. The result was to make them two- or three-page models of clarity, unlike illustrations here in Canada, which may run from 5 to 10 pages of columns, numbers, and confusing headings or titles.

At the very least, when you finish reading an illustration, you should know:

- cost of the premium;
- maximum and minimum premiums (if applicable);
- amount of the death benefits;
- projected cash value;
- projected dividends;
- administration and management costs the company charges;
- underlying assumptions for inflation, interest rates, and mortality rates for cash value and dividends;
- renewal options;
- convertibility;
- charges;
- guarantees.

You may also want to ask your agent if the illustration is current, using today's interest rates, for example; or whether the classification is the right one for you. For example, there is no point looking at an illustration for a non-smoker if you smoke—the premiums will be much too low. Are the premiums due monthly or annually? Will the company notify you if it changes any amounts that it has not guaranteed?

Don't be afraid to ask questions about the illustrations you are shown. After all, you wouldn't buy a car without knowing its age, mileage, warranty, and price. And remember that an illustration is not a legal document, nor is it legally binding. An illustration is just that—a "for instance"—and its only constant, as the saying goes, is change. Your costs and benefits may be higher or lower than those listed in the illustration because they are affected by the financial health of the company or, in the case of universal life insurance, by the status of your financial portfolio.

10. How do I know if the insurance company is sound?

The best way to check up on the health of life insurance companies is to regularly read the business sections of Canada's major daily newspapers. Most assign business reporters to cover the insurance industry or the financial services industry, which includes insurance. In any case, business sections report the rising and falling fortunes of insurance companies in Canada and offshore. You may want to pay attention to the news from abroad, as it sometimes affects the financial stability of companies in Canada.

Another way to find out if the insurance company will be able to pay future claims is to check reports from rating agencies, such as Moody's, Standard & Poors (both American), and TRAC, a division of A. M. Best Canada Ltd. (see "Consumer Resources" in Appendix A for contact information). These agencies assess a company's financial strength by looking at its surplus (assets, liabilities and surplus)—the money available for paying unexpected expenses and for its reserves, that crucial stash of $$$ used to pay your claims. Rating agencies also examine company profits and business strategies, as well as the quality of the organization's underlying assets, such as bonds, mortgages, and real estate investments. They run the numbers through the computers and come up with ratings ranging from A's (the best) through F's (same as when we were in school—a failing grade).

How good are the rating agencies? Canadian regulations for insurance differ from American rules, so the Canadian rating agency may be the best one to use. Also, some rating agencies, like some teachers, are more generous with their A's than others. So watch the trend: Have ratings for your insurance company gone up or down over time? If they've gone down, ask why.

11. What happens if my insurance company goes under?

While that is unlikely, it is certainly possible. Confederation Life of Canada was one of the largest life insurance companies in Canada, but it folded in 1995. Size doesn't matter; no company is too big to founder.

But there is protection for consumers. The life industry protects its clients through the Canadian Life and Health Insurance Compensation Corporation—CompCorp—a non-profit consumer protection plan. All life insurance companies doing business in Canada belong to CompCorp and contribute to it through assessments and, when needed, loans.

If your insurance company fails, CompCorp guarantees your coverage up to certain limits, as shown below. These limits apply to each policyholder and to each company. That means, if you have two life insurance policies, each with death benefits of $200,000 held by different companies, CompCorp will guarantee both policies.

The limits are:

- $200,000 for life insurance;
- $60,000 for guaranteed investment certificate-type products and for the cash values in life insurance policies;
- $60,000 for registered retirement savings plans (RRSPs) and registered retirement income funds (RRIFs) combined;
- $2,000 per month for annuities and disability income policies;
- $60,000 for other health benefits.

12. How do I choose an insurance provider?

The best life insurance provider is not your brother-in-law or sister, for two reasons. First, you may not want close relatives to know as much about you as is usually necessary to disclose when buying life insurance. Second, if you decide to switch companies or agents, family gatherings may start to feel more like the War of the Roses than a Walton family Christmas.

Similarly, you may not want to deal with the person who has been your parents' agent for 30 years, has been around since you were knee-high to a grasshopper and "knows" just what you need. You may want to look for a provider who is close to your own age—you can grow old together, and still have a good business relationship. You'll also want some experience working for you; that is, an agent or broker who has been selling life policies for a few years—you don't want to be someone's first customer. Often the best way to find the right individual is to ask trusted friends and associates, then approach "the chosen" to make presentations to you.

Life insurance can be sold through three major channels: agents, who are tied to one insurance company and sell only that company's products; direct-response insurers, who generally sell the products of their particular company over the telephone; and brokers, who sell products on behalf of a number of companies. Some call themselves life underwriters, financial planners, or financial consultants. Many people also have the option of buying group life insurance through their workplace or through a professional association to which they belong. (See chapter 1 for more information on how insurance is sold.)

Ask prospective insurance sellers about their training and qualifications, as well as affiliations to professional associations. Those with a CLU (Chartered Life Underwriter) or CH.F.C. (Chartered Financial Consultant) designation have made a commitment to the industry, themselves and their clients.

Industry associations include the Canadian Association of Insurance and Financial Advisors, and the Independent Life Insurance Brokers of Canada (see "Consumer Resources" in Appendix A for contact information). You should also know if your insurance provider is licensed in the province and can provide references from other clients.

13. When and how do I pay premiums? What happens if I don't or cannot pay my premium for a couple of months?

Life insurance premiums are generally paid annually, but may also be paid monthly, quarterly, or semi-annually. The life companies are happy to oblige. With universal life and certain whole life policies, you may also choose to accelerate your payments to pay off your policy faster.

Life Versus Vice: No Contest

"Although life insurance premiums can be reckoned a necessity
in anyone's budget, more money is spent per annum by
Canadians on the luxuries of alcoholic beverages and cigarettes
than is spent on the purchase of life insurance."
—Canadian Insurance *magazine, early 1940s*

As for not paying your premium "for a couple of months," this will put your policy in a very bad place, called "lapsed." If you can't pay for a month, that's a little different (and a lot better), since there is a 30-day grace period after the due date to pay a monthly life premium; after that, "termination." And if you happen to terminate (die) during this time, the death benefit is paid, but any outstanding premium is deducted from that payment.

If you've been delinquent for up to two years, you can still work your way back into the good graces of the life insurer by paying the overdue premiums plus interest. However, you may have to take a medical or provide "satisfactory medical evidence" to pass muster.

You probably have some built-in safeguards against non-payment of premiums right in your own policy, so check it out. As the Canadian Life and Health Insurance Association (CLHIA) says, there are three "non-forfeiture options" in permanent life policies (but not term policies). CLHIA's *Guide to Buying Life Insurance* describes these safeguards which, if you have them, are noted in your insurance contract:

1. Automatic premium loan: The cash values already built up in your policy may be used to pay the premiums. Obviously, there are limits, depending on how much the cash values have grown over the years. But it does mean that you won't have to forfeit your policy immediately if you are unable to meet a premium. It gives you breathing space to decide what to do about maintaining your coverage.

2. Reduced paid-up permanent policy: Your cash value is used to buy a lesser amount of permanent insurance. No further premium payments are required.

3. Extended term insurance: Your cash value is used to buy the same amount of insurance you currently have, but as term insurance. No further premiums are required. As the new policy is term, it expires at some point. How long it continues depends on how much cash value is available: the higher the cash value, the longer the extended term that can be bought.

14. What happens when I apply for life insurance?

First, don't be in a hurry to sign up. Be prepared to talk to several providers to get a good idea of what's available—a huge array that can be overwhelm-

Yes, But Did You Inhale?

Q. You used to smoke marijuana, 10 years ago when you were in college. But how do you answer a question on your life insurance application that asks: "Did you ever smoke marijuana or take any hallucinogenic drugs?"

A. Answer this question honestly! It's rare that a risky behaviour from your past will cause you to be penalized with a higher premium now. And if you do somehow get caught not telling the truth on a life insurance application, either before or after the policy is issued, the insurance company has grounds to reject coverage or even deny the claim.

ing at first. Be patient, and don't be enticed into filling out the application for insurance until you feel comfortable with your choice of policy and the person selling it. You should be in the driver's seat.

Then, when you do sit down to complete the application, be prepared for a rigorous examination of your health, lifestyle, and habits.

Health questions are abundant, as you might expect, ranging from family history of diseases, through the full complement of emotional and physical disorders. One questionnaire even asks about any consultations or checkups with alternative health care providers, such as herbalists, acupuncturists, homeopaths, and naturopaths.

The lifestyle questions usually include one like this: "Have you ever used hallucinogenic, stimulant, narcotic, sedative or tranquilizing drugs except as prescribed by a physician?" If yes, be prepared to provide details—drugs and dates, etc.

Any past unlawful conduct is also scrutinized: "Have you ever been charged with any criminal offence?"

Alcohol use is probed as well: "Have you ever received advice, counselling or treatment for alcohol use?"

Smoking and driving history are also on the quiz, but are usually more time-restricted than the "have you ever?" questions. For example: "Have you used any form of tobacco, marijuana, nicotine products or nicotine substitutes in the last 12 months?"

Even your leisure activities come under the microscope. A few typical questions include:

- "During the past two years, have you participated in any hazardous activities, such as auto racing, parachute jumping, scuba diving?"

If your answer is yes, prepare for many more questions, like:

- "As a scuba diver, do you engage in ice diving, wreck diving, rescue diving, cave diving, night diving, salvage work, search work?"
- "Do you ever dive alone?"

Insurance salespeople want you to sign on the dotted line, of course, but you should never feel any pressure to do so.

Once you have filled out the application, an independent examiner will likely telephone you on behalf of the insurance company within 10 days to two weeks to verify the information you've provided.

Depending on your age, the state of your health, and the size of the policy, you may or may not need a full physical. If you're young and able and

SCENARIO

Sitting The Exam—Or Not

Q. You're buying insurance for the first time, and wonder: Will I have to undergo a rigorous medical examination before my application will be accepted?

A. Not always. The older you are, or the higher the value of the policy you're purchasing, the more likely the insurance company will want to know you're in good health now, and require a thorough medical exam, often by a doctor of the insurer's choice. If you're young and not asking for a lot of coverage, you may have your blood pressure, pulse, and other simple tests done by a paramedic or nurse at your home or office.

not asking for much coverage, your own doctor's assessment of your health over a period of years will likely be acceptable. A megabuck policy, and you'll be put through your paces thoroughly by at least one physician endorsed by the insurance company, including the gamut of cardiovascular examinations, chest X-ray, blood and urine tests.

As for the health information the insurance agent gleans from you and your doctor, an abbreviated version of it may go into a pool of data shared among more than 700 life companies across North America. Actually, only one in 10 policyholders has a such a file, which is administered by a non-profit organization called the Medical Information Bureau (MIB). The purpose of this Bureau is to help protect against insurance fraud. Confidentiality is assured, but if you are concerned that there may be a file on you and, if that is the case, you want to know what's in it, contact the Bureau and ask for disclosure (see "Consumer Resources" in Appendix A for contact information).

15. What happens if I make a mistake on my application?

If you make an "honest error"—or even a dishonest one—on your application form for life insurance, better let the company know as soon as possible. As the Canadian Life and Health Insurance Association (CLHIA) says: "Failure to provide complete and accurate information could invalidate your insurance coverage. Occasionally, an applicant may discover that a fact has been omitted or innocently misrepresented on the application. In that case, the insurance company should be notified immediately so that any necessary adjustment can be made."

If, however, the error stays put and is discovered at the claims stage, the company can take punitive action based on the nature of the "misinformation." If your age was reported incorrectly, CLHIA says, "the insurance company will usually adjust the benefits accordingly and pay the claim. However, if smoking status or other vital information has been misrepresented, the insurer may deny the claim and pay only a refund of premiums."

Honesty is the best policy. However: "By law, a life insurance policy, including the application, is incontestable after two years. After that time, except for fraud (that is, a deliberate misstatement of fact), a company can-

From Funeral Director To Deep-Sea Diver

Q. You already have a life insurance policy, but you recently switched professions, from funeral director to deep-sea diver. Do you have to inform your insurer?

A. Surprisingly, the answer is no. You would think that a life insurance company would be anxious to know if you're taking more risks with the very thing it's insuring, but that's not the case. Dive away! (However, if you're a deep-sea diver at the time of application, don't tell the insurer you're an undertaker in the hope that you'll save a little money on the premium.)

not deny a claim because the information you provided was incorrect or incomplete."

Does all this mean your little white lie will slip by after two years? The key phrase here is "deliberate misstatement." So, better to be honest, even if some questions on the application make you wonder if the truth, the whole truth, and nothing but the truth will still allow you to get the most insurance coverage for the lowest premium.

Provide as much detail as possible about these situations. This allows the underwriter to make the most appropriate decision: to accept your application at the standard rate, accept it at an increased rate, or decline you for coverage.

So, will "yes" to a question like "Have you ever smoked marijuana?"— which may seem like ancient history if you had a toke or two 10 years ago in college—put your application at risk? Or if you admit you're an alcoholic, but you've had treatment and have faithfully attended Alcholics Anonymous for the past eight years? Most likely you will still be classified as a standard risk, and get the regular rate. Only about 6 per cent of all applicants are judged to be higher risks.

He Should've Invested In
Life Insurance

Suicide Over Real Estate Losses
"J.S. Kyle of Chesterville (Ont.) suicided in Saskatoon, on
February 17th, owing to financial troubles in real estate
speculation. He wouldn't have suicided had his money been
locked up in insurance policies. Real estate speculation has
wrecked many homes. Life insurance never wrecked a single
home. It has kept millions intact."
—Canadian Insurance *magazine, March 5, 1913*

16. What happens if I "forget" to tell my insurer I bungee jump for a living?

Really not a good idea. Your policy application will ask for your occupation and, as question 15 notes, a deliberate "misstatement" can make your coverage null and void.

Strangely, if you buy a life insurance policy while working as an accountant, and then change careers to something much more adventuresome (and perilous), like leading mountain-climbing expeditions in the Himalayas, that's different. You don't even need to inform your life insurer, and there's no penalty if the insurer "finds out."

Similarly, you may never have been a drinker before signing up for life insurance, then suddenly discover a mad passion for Singapore Slings. Doesn't matter, at least not to the insurance company. Once the policy is in your pocket, you can take all the risks in the world and you'll still be covered.

17. What happens if I commit suicide?

We hope you are never in such dire straits, and, if you are, that you find the help you need to see you through to better days.

That said, suicide is definitely not recommended during the first two years of a life policy; in fact, by law, killing yourself within this time period will nullify the death benefit. (If you thought *you* were depressed, imagine how your would-be beneficiary will feel with a 23-month-old life policy for a million bucks in your name...)

If death occurs during the first 24 months after your policy has been issued, a physician must sign a statement certifying that the death was not suicide in order for the death claim to be valid—and paid.

18. What happens when I die?

From a life insurance standpoint, it's the responsibility of your beneficiary to set the claims process in motion. And the process is usually a very simple one: the beneficiary contacts the insurance agent or broker, or, in the case of group life insurance, the benefits administrator for the employer, union, or other association. The insurance company usually provides a form for the claim. This, appropriately filled out, plus a death certificate or doctor's statement, is usually all that is needed.

Most life companies, after receiving this documentation, will pay the death claim within 10 to 20 days. Some circumstances, such as the need to investigate the cause of death, may slow down this process, however. If your beneficiary thinks the claim is not being paid promptly enough, he or she can seek help from the consumer assistance centre at the Canadian Life and Health Insurance Association, or the superintendent of insurance in the province where the policy was issued (see "Consumer Resources" in Appendix A for contact information).

SCENARIO

Making A Contingency Plan

Q. You and your spouse, who also happens to be your named beneficiary, both die at the same time in a car accident.

What happens to your death benefit?

A. It goes to your estate, unless you have named a "contingent"—or "alternate"—beneficiary.

---

19. What are living benefits?

Living benefits—also called viaticals—provide some payout of the life policy before one's death, as a result of specific "occurrences," such as a diagnosis of cancer, heart disease, dementia, or in the event of a stroke or paraplegia. A living benefit is actually a loan against the death benefit. This can be very helpful in paying health care and other costs associated with a serious illness or accident. The company recovers the living benefit payout, plus interest on the "loan," from the death benefit when you die. This might be a "rider" or option you choose as part of your life policy.

20. What other riders and options are available?

There are many, but three of the more common ones include the following:

• *Double indemnity* is the old-fashioned phrase for what is now commonly known as the *accidental death benefit*. It doubles the death benefit if your demise is caused accidentally. Sounds good, but if you have sufficient insurance coverage in place anyway, your dependents don't need twice as much. The truth is, less than 10 per cent of all deaths of 25- to 65-year-olds result from accidents.

• *Waiver of premium* continues to pay your life insurance premium if you become disabled. However, the definition of waiver of premium is usually so restrictive—"totally and permanently disabled"—that it's a rare claimant who benefits. You might want to consider buying a disability policy instead (see chapter 6).

• *Guaranteed insurability* allows you to buy additional insurance at designated times during the life of the policy at standard rates, without having to submit to a medical. The extra insurance that you can buy, and when you can buy it, are specified when you opt for this rider. However, the extra cost may not justify this option. It might be smarter to buy the additional insurance when you purchase the policy in the first place.

Ask your insurance provider about other available options.

21. I am middle-aged and don't think I will "pass" a life company medical exam. Should I buy the kind of life insurance advertised on television, which doesn't require a medical exam?

It's probably a better idea to check with several insurance agents, brokers, and direct-response insurers (see question 12) first. The insurance advertised on television, through telemarketing, and by direct mail, which promises that you "won't be refused," generally offers very little coverage at a much higher per-thousand cost than conventional insurance. It also limits the death benefit in the early years of the policy. Of course, if you don't qualify in the regular market, then it's up to you. But comparison-shop first.

22. What if I change my mind two weeks after I sign up for a policy?

Better hustle a little faster and make it 10 days. By law, everyone who signs up for life insurance in Canada has 10 days after receipt to examine the policy and send it back if it's not wanted. This is called the "right of recission." Satisfaction or your money back.

Just make sure you get the policy in hand promptly, because it's pretty hard to rescind unless you send it back.

CAUTION

Before You Replace...

Before you decide to replace an existing policy with a new one, see if you can upgrade the old one to meet your changing needs. This may save you a lot of heartache... and money. If you do decide to change policies, make sure the new one is in force before cancelling the old one.

---

23. What if I want to switch from whole life to term after six or seven years of paying for whole? What should I know before I replace the policy?

You'd be wise to ask for a projection of the values of your existing policy from your insurance company before jumping ship. This "illustration" will give you some idea of the projected cash values or death benefits of this policy. It will also disclose the "assumptions" used—which values are guaranteed and which values are non-guaranteed projections.

In deciding whether to replace an existing policy with a new policy, you should consider the following:

- What are the current cash values under the existing policy?
- What amount would be received on an after-tax basis if the policy was surrendered (income tax may be payable on a portion of the surrender value)?
- How is the cash value projected to grow, and what sort of investment return does this represent?
- How is the death benefit expected to grow?
- What are the current and future premiums payable?
- Can you re-qualify on a medical basis for new insurance? (If you do decide to replace the insurance, always have the new policy issued first and then surrender the older policy.)
- What premiums would be payable for new insurance (since premiums would be based on your current age, smoking status, and medical condition)?

24. Can I get life insurance from an organization other than a life insurance company?

Definitely. These days, you can purchase many different types of insurance—life, health, disability, travel, homeowners, automobile—through memberships in professional organizations, unions, university alumni groups, and other organizations (although it is still "underwritten" by a life insurance company). If it seems to you that everyone is getting into insurance these days, you're just about right. It's good for you as a consumer, but it takes time, and means doing your homework, to get the best coverage for the best price.

25. What are those "vanishing premiums" that we have heard so much about?

Very simply, this means using your "dividends" and "paid-up additions" to pay off your policy early, say, after 15 or 20 years. (Remember "dividend" and "paid-up addition"? See question 7.) But it's not quite so simple in reality, since your premium may not "vanish" when you expect it to. Policy dividends are not guaranteed, so a fixed date when premiums will disappear can't be, either. Be sure to get a full explanation of vanishing premiums from your insurance provider.

Checklist

Questions to ask your insurance provider before you purchase your insurance

1. What is guaranteed in the policy and what isn't? (This should include all aspects of the policy: the premiums you pay, benefits you receive, how and when "riders" apply, and so on.)

2. How long has your prospective insurance representative been in business? What education and professional accreditation does this individual have? How long has the insurance company been in business?

3. Comparing term insurance policies is much easier than comparing permanent policies. But even with term policies, remember to ask what your renewal rates will be 10, 20, and 30 years down the line. What is the difference between various policies you're considering?

4. Comparing permanent insurance policies is much more challenging than comparing term policies, since there are so many variations. Here's where insurance company jargon can get a little mind-boggling. What is the "interest-adjusted net cost index"? And the "interest-adjusted net payment index"? Good questions, and you need to get both sets of indices from your insurance provider in order to compare similar policies from different life companies. Again, get a good explanation of these concepts from your representative.

5. Policy "illustrations" can be a minefield. Ask very specific questions about the assumptions in the illustrations you're shown, such as:
   - If there is an investment segment to the policy, what rate of return is assumed? What if the rate is lower? Higher?
   - Is the death benefit guaranteed? (You may assume it is, but ask to be certain.)
   - Will premiums fluctuate? If so, under what circumstances?

Keywords

Beneficiary	The person named in the policy who receives the death benefit.
Cash value	The part of a permanent insurance policy that builds up over time. Policyholders may choose to cash in the policy if they no longer require the life coverage, but this forfeits the death benefit.
Convertibility	The ability to change from one type of life policy to another without evidence of insurability, i.e., having to undergo a medical examination.
Death benefit	The money paid out on a life policy after a death claim is approved.
Guaranteed renewal	A promise by the insurance company that a policy will be renewed without penalty or a medical exam after the term has expired. The renewal rate can also be guaranteed.
Rider	Optional protection on a life policy purchased as an extra, such as the "accidental death benefit."
Term insurance	A life insurance policy issued for a specific period, say 5, 10, 20, or even 100 years.
Universal life insurance	A type of policy that combines term insurance with flexible premiums and a separate savings program directed, to some extent, by the policyholder.
Whole life insurance	A policy with a cash value component that protects for one's entire life.

5

health insurance

Private group health insurance through your workplace

Individual private health insurance

Critical illness insurance

What to do when you have an insurance claim

Why Private Health Insurance?

THE HEALTH CARE SYSTEM IN CANADA ensures that virtually everyone living here has access to medical services in any part of the country. You likely have a provincial health card that gets you into doctors' visits and hospital, and covers various blood tests, X-rays, and other medical procedures. As lauded as the Canadian system is, however, it doesn't cover everything. With a few exceptions, provincial plans don't cover dental care or pay for medications. They also won't pay for glasses or contact lenses. Many of us turn to private plans purchased by our employers or, increasingly, to individual private health care plans.

As with all kinds of insurance, if you are considering private health insurance you've probably played the "what if" game: What if I never work for a company that offers health and dental benefits? What if I continue to be a contract employee but need to address some long-standing dental needs? What if I finally set up my own small company but then develop a serious illness? What if I need extra help at home after a hospital stay? What if I take a leave of absence to finish my studies and I have to have a root canal? Private health insurance can relieve some of these worries. You'll still have to consider the monthly premiums, the extent of coverage, and whether your medical conditions will be accepted.

Unlike emergency health insurance you may consider purchasing when you go away on vacation (see chapter 7), regular individual health insurance is designed for the day-to-day troubles, surgeries, and treatments that, while routine, can add up to big bills. Responding in part to the changing workforce where more people are working on short-term contracts or for themselves, insurers are offering a variety of health care packages to cover the needs of individuals. What started as a basic plan has become a virtual buffet of services where consumers can choose which benefits they want and need. If you work for a company that offers health care but not dental care benefits, for instance, purchase your own dental benefits. If you have prescription needs but can't afford a full package, choose a basic health plan including a drug plan, and skip the dental or vision portions. If you have a growing family and want as much coverage as possible, order the works. There are also some packages designed for health care catastrophes that would pay much more than the regular plans for serious illnesses that

Sample The Smorgasbord

Q. You are in dire need of an extended health care and dental plan, but you don't need vision care or a drug plan. Do you have to take the whole kit and caboodle?

A. No. Most private health plans offered today allow you to choose from a smorgasbord of offerings, so you can tailor your coverage to meet your needs.

would result in substantial drug or therapy charges. The choices are improving, and, for some people the cost of health insurance can be used as a tax deduction.

Of course, wanting insurance and getting it are two different things. Insurers will have you think that everything is simple. One brochure insists you can enroll in a plan in five easy steps and less than 10 minutes. Well, maybe it's that simple if you are young, in excellent health, want very basic service, and have no interest in the details. For the rest of us, it makes more sense to pick up the phone and ask questions. Lots of them. You won't want to be sorting out misunderstandings when you are sick. Take care of it before you sign up, and keep notes, so you will remember your understanding of what you bought.

How are you feeling?

Of greatest concern to insurance companies offering health care packages is what they call "pre-existing conditions." Take a good hard look at your own health, because they will. Applying for insurance after your mammogram shows something suspicious may see you turned down or at least restricted in what you can buy. Generally, the healthier and younger you are when you approach a company, the better the rates and the more options you have. That said, if you do have a medical condition that is "under control," you may have no difficulties being approved. If you take medication to regulate an overactive thyroid, for instance, and that medication hasn't changed in many years, it won't likely be a concern for the insurer. If your condition isn't stable and your drug and treatment needs change frequently, the insurer may consider your risk to be too high to take on. Sure, they'll sell you vision care and dental care packages, but they won't want to be on the hook for all the expensive medications and hospital visits they think you will likely need. Pre-existing conditions can apply to dental plans too.

No matter what kind of policy you rely on, private or government, bare-bones or high-end, you could be out of pocket if you have a health care problem. Many plans have deductibles that require you to pay for the first few hundred dollars of expenses, for instance, before the insurance kicks in. Others have limits on how much they will cover, giving you some help but not the full cost of your treatments. Most packages are designed to cover the average healthy person's needs. They can take the sting out of the final bills but won't cover everything. Catastrophic or critical illness plans may be of more value to protect your life savings and credit limit from being swallowed up by a very serious illness.

Government help

If you can't afford access to private health care, if the plan you have can't meet your real needs, or if you are over age 65, you may be eligible for government support. In some provinces, if a large portion of your income is going to pay for medication, you may be eligible for assistance. You may

TIP

Keep It Handy

Keep your medical insurance plan number and telephone number with your health card. If you are ever taken to hospital and need extra services, you won't have to send someone home to hunt for it.

A Clever Deduction

Keep copies of all your receipts. What isn't covered by a government or private health insurance plan can be submitted with your income tax return and may be used as a deduction. Self-employed people can deduct premiums for health and dental insurance.

also be able to use what comes out of your pocket for medical care and drugs as a tax deduction at the end of the year. Hang on to the receipts and any statements that come back from your insurance company to show how much you spent. The insurance deductibles can be included in your tax statements.

Frequently Asked Questions ... About Health Insurance

1. Do I have to have health insurance?

There is no legal requirement for you to have private health insurance, but you can probably imagine the costs without it. As long as you have status in your province of residence, you are entitled to benefits under your provincial government plan. Everyone—even babies—must apply in order to participate in the provincial plan, but your current state of health is of no concern. You are covered whether you are terminally ill or in the peak of health. Once a number and card have been issued to you, you will be able to access health care across Canada. Some provinces will, however, limit coverage payments to those from out-of-province.

While basic health needs are covered by government plans, with a few exceptions, most individuals are still responsible for buying their own medicines and paying for their own dental care. You may decide you can't afford to pay for a private system and either don't have a job or don't have a job that includes a health care package as a benefit. That often changes how we manage our care. How long do you go with a cavity when you pay the dentist out of your own pocket? What kind of medicine do you choose without a drug plan? Do you fill every prescription your doctor writes? Do you skip doses to make your medication last? Are you jeopardizing your health because you can't afford the treatments? Ultimately, it is up to you and your ability to pay for health care.

A special note to new immigrants to Canada. There is often a waiting period between your arrival and when your provincial health plan coverage begins. Some companies offer insurance specifically to cover that gap. It usually comes under the category of visitor or travel insurance (see chapter 7). If you decide to head back before your policy runs out, you may be eligible for a refund, so if you're a visitor, you needn't feel you are wasting money if you are generous in your estimate of how long you'll be in Canada.

You usually are required to purchase the insurance before you land in Canada, so plan ahead.

2. Doesn't my government plan cover everything?

Government health plans cover the basics that most of us would need. They pay for most doctors' appointments and services, hospital care, bandages,

---

SCENARIO

Filling The Gap For New Canadians

Q. Your sister is about to immigrate to Canada from Scotland. Will she need private health insurance?
A. Yes, most likely. There is usually a waiting period (check with the provincial health ministry to see how long) between the immigrant's arrival and the time that individual's provincial health plan coverage kicks in. Some companies offer insurance specifically to cover that gap; it usually comes under the category of visitor or travel insurance.

---

medications administered while you are in hospital, nursing care, X-rays, ultrasounds, blood tests, and other diagnostic work. Some kinds of treatments and services that might appear to be in the same category are not covered. For instance, cosmetic surgery is generally not covered, unless it is performed as the result of an accident or is deemed "necessary" by the surgeon, and some fertility treatments are not covered. Your grandmother's flu shot may be covered because she is elderly, but yours may not be because you are not in an age group at high risk from flu. Private plans will not pick up everything that the government plan excludes, but it's always worth asking. Some blood tests, for example, that are not paid for under government plans may be covered by private insurance, depending on your age and medical history. Some provincial plans limit the number of eye examinations you may have at public expense in a certain period of time. Private plans may pay for further tests.

The most commonly used services that are not included in government plans are dental care and drugs. There have been many debates about whether there should be socialized dental and drug programs, and some provinces do provide assistance to their most needy residents. Most of us turn to private plans purchased by our employers or, increasingly, to individual private health care plans.

3. What do private health insurance plans cover?

The plans you might be most familiar with through your employer kick in after the provincial plan's limits have been reached. The provincial plan will pay for a hospital room. The private plan will get you into a semi-private or private room. This feature might be less important today, with hospital rooms usually holding no more than four patients anyway. The provincial plan will get you to a doctor who may write a prescription; the private plan will help you pay for the medication at the pharmacy. The provincial plan will pay for major surgery to your jaw in hospital; the private plan will pay for treatments in the dentist's chair. Private plans will also include what's called accidental death and dismemberment insurance, which would provide a lump-sum payment should you die, become paralyzed, or lose a limb. Some private plans include money for buying glasses or contact lenses.

Group health insurance plans through work often also include disability plans that will provide you with an income if you become disabled and are unable to work (see chapter 6). Some employers purchase particularly enhanced benefits packages as a lure to attract and keep good employees. If your company plan is a good one, keep it in mind before you ever consider quitting in a huff. A group plan spreads the risk over a larger number of people who are working and who are usually under age 65. That gives the insurer clues about the potential cost of servicing claims and allows for more features in the plan. A really good group plan might include adult orthodontics, for instance. It would be very difficult to get that kind of coverage on your own. Simply put, there is strength in numbers, and buying in bulk usually reduces the cost.

4. What is extended health care?

Extended health care is meant to pick up where your government plan ends. In some provinces, a ride in an ambulance will cost you money whether you ordered it yourself or were picked up unconscious following an accident. Extended health benefits would cover that expense. Prosthetic appliances, and medical supplies and equipment also fall under extended health. In addition, extended health care covers services you might need for a longer period of time than your government plan will support. For instance, depending on the plan, it might cover physiotherapy, home care and nursing, visits to a psychologist or speech therapist or a registered massage therapist, acupuncturist, or chiropractor. Some of these services

CAUTION

You Can't Take It With You

Your employer-sponsored health plan is not portable; it doesn't go with you if you leave your job. Therefore, if you have a good plan at your workplace, don't quit without considering the implications and alternatives.

might be covered by your provincial plan, with limits. The private plans also have limits. You'll find a lifetime maximum for services that could be plus or minus $50,000 to $100,000, depending on the package you have purchased. There will also be limits on how much can be spent for each visit. Don't expect those limits to necessarily match the cost of what you pay. One company, for example, offers $15 for a therapeutic massage. It may be difficult to find a therapist who is willing to offer even minimal service for that price. There may be limits on the number of times the company will pay for visits to a therapist as well. Ten speech pathology sessions in a year may not move you along as fast as your potential. Even if you have planned in advance and purchased insurance, always be prepared to be out of pocket if you have a problem. Nothing covers everything. If such a product did exist, the price would likely be so high that no one would buy it.

5. I have a plan through my job. Shouldn't that be enough?

If it's a good one, as we noted above, yes it should. But check it out and know what is included. The plan's efficacy depends on the agreement your employer has struck with the insurer and how many benefits are included in the package. A small employer, or a cheap plan, might not offer as many benefits as you would want access to. Do you have a large family with vision problems? You might want a plan that includes coverage for glasses. Do you or does someone in your family suffer from an illness that requires expensive medications? You won't want a plan with tight limits or high deductibles on drugs. Are you particular about your privacy, and your company plan doesn't include semi-private or private coverage in hospital? You might want to buy up with your own separate plan.

Many employers are working out flexible options within their plans too. With two-career families, there may be reason to opt out of one spouse's plan in favor of the other's, or take one benefit from one employer and another from the next. Ask questions.

The downside to plans from work is that they are dependent on your employment and are not portable. You can't take it with you if you change jobs. A private plan is yours to keep for as long as you pay the premiums.

Know Your Limits

Most private health plans have some limits. These will vary,
depending on the package you buy, but they may not match what
you have to pay for certain services. Be prepared to pay the
excess out of pocket.

6. Where do I start looking for private insurance?

To get an idea of the full range of companies out there, look in the Yellow Pages under "Insurance—Life and Health." If you want detailed information to get you started, watch for pamphlets at pharmacies. Some companies arrange to have them displayed in drugstores, and have probably paid a fee to do so. Don't take the display to be an endorsement by your pharmacist. If you have access, look on the Internet. Some quick comparisons can be made of the larger companies with Web sites. Some insurers will even allow you to apply for insurance by e-mail. If you have an insurance broker or agent, ask if he or she carries health insurance, remembering that brokers and agents do not necessarily cover every company's products. If you don't have an agent or broker, ask your friends for recommendations. Since you will have to discuss some pretty personal information, you'll want a broker or agent you trust and feel comfortable with.

You may also be able to buy health coverage through a professional association or other group to which you belong, and take advantage of a group rate.

Some insurance companies offer packages through employers for contract workers. These packages are similar to group plans, but may not, for example, cover anyone working less than 20 hours a week. Each province has different laws that stipulate when employees must be offered company benefits. Depending on where you live, you may be able to participate in a group plan, even if you are working part-time.

7. How do I decide what I need?

Weigh the options and consider your needs, both today and in the future. Do you wear glasses? Does anyone in your family? Does your family history indicate that you likely will? If so, you might want to consider a plan that includes coverage for eyewear. Do you plan on having children? That almost guarantees a hospital stay. Would you want a semi-private room? Do you have children who might need regular dental work? Could you afford to pay for it yourself? Do you have a condition that requires regular or expensive medication? Can you afford the cost of that? Will your health insurance company cover drugs for a pre-existing condition? For example, if you are diabetic and require insulin, your condition would be taken into account in the underwriting process. Will the company cover your medication and any future complications? You will also have to decide how much you can afford in premiums.

8. Are there bells and whistles?

Yes, to a degree. Some companies offer newsletters with tips on how to maintain good health. The same type of information is available for free in some pharmacies. Other companies provide access to a telephone helpline staffed by nurses offering medical information. Again, some pharmacies offer similar services. You could also purchase insurance that would give you cash should you be hospitalized. This covers personal expenses that are tough to avoid while you are in hospital: the forgotten toothbrush, your favourite soap, television or telephone rentals.

TIP

Keep Up With The Times

Review your plan from time to time. Benefits change and so does your health. There may be new programs available to suit your specific needs.

9. I am self-employed. Can I buy my own plan?

Yes, but be prepared to pay a price for it. Like many products, when you buy in bulk, you save money; when you purchase single units, it costs more. So you won't be able to buy as much as a large employer does at the same cost. Rates range from about $25 to $100 a month, depending on your age and the plan you purchase. Generally, the older the applicant, the higher the prices. Basic drug plans are available at the lower end of the scale, with plans combining drugs, dental, vision, extended health care, travel health coverage, and accidental death and dismemberment at the higher end of the price range. For some categories, monthly premiums charged to seniors are higher, but so are some of the benefits.

In addition, some insurers offer à la carte service for other coverage you may wish to add on or buy separately. For instance, you may not need ongoing benefits like drug, dental, and vision care, but you would like an extended health care package to cover you in the event of a health catastrophe.

The key phrase in most of these packages is "some conditions apply." Those conditions may not allow you to get what you need, and at a price you can afford. On the other hand, it might be better than no coverage at all. You must weigh the risks of developing a health problem with your ability to pay for care.

Individual health plans may be of interest to others besides the self-employed. For example, you may want more than your employee plan

---

CAUTION

Not So Simple

Some insurers will lead you to believe in their promotional materials that buying health insurance is as easy as filling out an application and sending in a cheque. Not! Your application still has to be approved before a policy will be issued. If you have what insurers call a "pre-existing condition," you may not pass muster. Beware the phrase "Some conditions apply." Ask questions!

offers. You may be taking a sabbatical from work and need temporary coverage, or you may be retired without access to adequate health insurance.

10. Can I buy health insurance like I would buy a pair of shoes, or must I apply for it?

Despite what some advertisements and brochures say, you must apply for health insurance. A lot of promotional material will have you think that, after filling out a brief form and sending in a cheque, you're covered. Not so. The fine print will tell you that what you have filled out is not a contract, and that a policy will be issued after your application has been approved.

For some of the very basic plans and services, you may not have to fill out a medical form, and coverage is pretty much guaranteed when you send in your payment and completed application. Those plans protect the insurance company through low limits on what can be claimed. For instance, you may have access to payment for drugs, but to a maximum of $250 in a year. If you rarely see a pharmacist, and even then only for temporary problems such as antibiotics for a throat infection, that amount should do the trick. If you are a serious migraine sufferer, $250 might cover one month of medications. Plans that offer greater benefits will require you to fill out a form that asks for age, height, weight, and whether you've lost or gained weight in the last year. If you have, they'll want to know why. They will also ask whether you have ever been treated for, or have even talked to a doctor about, a variety of disorders, including back pain, headaches, high blood pressure, heart disease, cancer, diabetes, asthma, alcohol or drug abuse, or mental problems, among others. They will ask about how you were treated for the ailment and for how long. They will also want to know what medications you are taking and whether you are scheduled for hospitalization or for treatment with medications within the next few months. Again, you won't likely be able to get coverage for treatments that are already scheduled.

11. Are there restrictions on who can apply for health insurance?

Anyone may apply for insurance, but there are restrictions on who will be accepted and for what coverage. If you have a medical condition that requires regular medication, that particular condition may be excluded from coverage, at least for the time being. The theory is that you can't buy fire insurance while your house is burning, so you can't insure against a medical condition that is already evident. Of course, there are always exceptions, so don't feel that you can't try. A good example is pregnancy. Some companies will offer limited health insurance to pregnant women if they apply early in the pregnancy. If you are HIV positive, you won't likely be offered health insurance at all. An insurer would expect that your needs for expensive medications, therapies, and treatments would be too high and almost a certainty.

You must be a resident of Canada and be covered by a provincial health plan.

12. How much do I have to tell them?

Pretty much everything the insurer asks for. You must disclose pre-existing conditions so that the insurer's financial risk in taking you on can be assessed. Remember, there is no law that says a company must insure you. It's a business, and if you are likely to cost the insurer a lot of money, it's likely to say no thank you. You must explain what treatments you have been undergoing, what medications you have been on, whether any of those medications have changed recently, and what medical conditions you have. If you are not forthcoming or if you tell an outright lie about your state of health and you subsequently have to file a claim, your application will be con-

---

SCENARIO

Acceptance Not Guaranteed

Q. You are taking medication for a heart condition. Do you qualify for private health insurance?
A. It depends. If your condition has been stable for at least a few years, you might qualify, but don't count on it. Sure, you'll be able to get a vision care or dental plan, but maybe not a drug or extended health care plan.

Nothing But The Truth

Don't conveniently "forget" to tell the insurance company about your recent bout with back pain when you are applying for coverage. If you have another one and the insurance company finds out it wasn't your first, your application will be considered fraudulent and your claim denied.

sidered fraudulent and your claim will be denied. If you lie in the claims process, fabricating receipts or claiming for things that didn't happen, not only will your claim not be covered, you could face criminal charges as well. Insurers are becoming increasingly less tolerant of such "nuisances," even the little white lies. In short, failure to disclose the truth is not worth the risk.

13. Will I have to undergo a medical examination?

Generally, no. Unlike life insurance and disability insurance (see chapters 4 and 6), health insurance tends to have fairly strict limits on what is covered and for how much money. You either have a prescription for medication or you don't. The drug is either covered or it's not. You are either in a semi-private hospital room or a ward. There are fewer gray areas. Completing a medical questionnaire is usually all that's required of you and, for some policies, you may not have to fill out a medical form at all.

14. Why would the insurance company turn me down?

If you have what is referred to as a pre-existing condition, the insurer may believe that your likelihood of suffering an illness is too high a risk to take on. For instance, if you have been diagnosed with cancer in the past three years (perhaps longer with some companies), your likelihood of claiming for large drug expenses may be very high and beyond the insurer's risk threshold. In that case, the insurer might see it as insurance, not for an unexpected illness, but for a guaranteed one. The insurer also needs to assess the risk of you requiring support in order to sort out how much to charge for a policy in your name. Each company is different, so if you don't have success with one, you may want to try another.

15. Is there any way to cut the cost?

Check out any associations in which you have a membership. Sometimes university alumni associations, unions, or professional clubs arrange to have group insurance available for individual members. The price might be lower, although the plan might not be what you are after.

Take care of yourself. The fewer ailments you have, the better the risk you are and the lower the price you will be charged for coverage. As with automobile insurance (see chapter 3), where good drivers pay less, non-smokers, for instance, pay less for health insurance (all things being equal). If you do have a medical condition, follow your physician's advice to help keep it stable.

Check out companies that offer choices in plans. You may be able to pick the services you want without having to pay for those you are less likely to use to the max. You may need help with dental care, but not need drug benefits, for instance.

16. Is health insurance considered a business expense?

The 1998 federal budget allowed self-employed people to deduct premiums for health and dental insurance, so, yes, you can recoup part of the costs. On the other hand, disability insurance premiums are not tax deductible if the benefits are intended to be tax-free (see chapter 6). If you do become disabled, you probably wouldn't want to give up part of your benefits to income tax, so you might be better off not using it as a deduction now to protect the full amount later.

Critical Illness/Long-Term Care Insurance

17. Generations of my family have been financially wiped out paying for care as they suffered through the effects of cancer. Can I get help for that?

A relatively new form of insurance called "critical illness insurance" is available for just that purpose. It provides money when you need it to pay for care while you are alive. Insurers are finding that many people who wouldn't consider life insurance are looking at critical illness insurance instead. For some people, it might make more sense to apply for something that will help them while they are still alive, rather than providing for their survivors. It is an expensive product, but has tremendous flexibility if you become critically ill. It provides a lump-sum payment for anything you wish. You don't have to get approval for expenditures or provide receipts. If you want to try alternative therapies or medications that aren't covered under government plans, use it for that. If you just need someone to clean your house and make your meals, the money is there. If you need a nanny to care for your children while you have and recover from treatments, you can pay for it through the lump sum. If you can't bear staring at the same four walls, you can buy a vacation package. Need to buy wigs and new clothing? Do it. No questions asked with this insurance.

If you die while the policy is still in force, a refund of premiums may be made to your named beneficiary.

18. Does critical illness insurance cover all illnesses?

These packages tend to cover cancers, heart disease, stroke, multiple sclerosis, blindness, organ transplants, kidney failure, and paralysis. Some specialty programs have emerged. One specifically deals with women's cancers, for instance. Few, if any, cover HIV.

TIP

History Can Repeat

Review your family history. Is there a history of diabetes, cancer, heart disease, migraine, or any other ailment? It might help you decide whether you can cover your own potential medical costs. If a serious disease like cancer, for example, runs in your family, you might want to consider applying for critical illness insurance.

19. How much does critical illness insurance cost?

As always, cost varies by person and by company. An average premium for a healthy non-smoking 35-year-old could be $25 to $30/month per $100,000 of coverage. For a 40-year-old non-smoker, look at about $20 a month for $25,000 or about $40 a month for $50,000 of coverage. Generally, the younger and healthier you are, the lower the premium.

20. What if I'm not critically ill, but need long-term care?

This may be a more common need as the population ages. Savvy financial planning in your youth will ensure that you have the funds to pay for a good retirement home or care facility. If your finances will need a boost when that need arises, you may want to consider long-term care insurance. It differs from other health insurance because it provides for care for a much longer period of time. In fact, most people who buy it opt for lifetime benefits. It will pay if you need help with personal or health care on a long-term basis at home or in a care facility. To receive the benefit, you require a physician's recommendation that care is medically necessary, which is usually the case if you've lost the ability to perform two or more activities of daily living. Perhaps you can no longer bathe yourself or prepare meals because of chronic arthritis, or Alzheimer's disease has left you without the ability to clean your home properly or make shopping decisions.

For a Cadillac plan, it could cost well over $1,000 a year in premiums, depending on your age. However, with some plans, there is a limit to the amount of premiums you pay (about 25 years maximum), and you may be able to add a provision that pays back your premiums if you die before accessing benefits. You may also be able to purchase this type of insurance well into your senior years, although the price goes up accordingly.

The Claims Scenario

21. My dental bill is so high I can't possibly pay it without my insurance money. Can my insurer be billed directly?

That depends on the company and the dentist. Some will allow for direct payment for dental work; most will reimburse you. Some dentists are prepared to work out a payment schedule, understanding that the timing of paycheques affects people's ability to pay large bills. That said, if you have the forms filled out properly and send them in directly to your insurer, payment should reach you in a few weeks. Check with friends on their experiences with insurers. You may find that some insurers are faster with the cheques than others. Of course, what the cheque covers may be more important in choosing an insurer.

22. What about hospital bills? Am I expected to be writing cheques from my bedside to cover the costs of care?

Hospital charges are usually billed directly to the insurer. When you are admitted to hospital, your insurance particulars are among the details the admitting staff request. With large or well-known companies, the hospital should have no problem submitting a claim directly. There may be exceptions, so don't take it as a guarantee. Generally, though, you shouldn't have to worry about the big bills.

Some pharmacies and insurance companies also have relationships that allow for direct billing for prescription drugs. It's a very handy service if your credit cards are at their maximum.

23. My husband and I are covered by plans at each of our jobs. Where do we send claims for our children?

Insurance companies have a protocol for dealing with such matters. Called "Coordination of Benefits," the guidelines help insurers decide who will pay first. Call your insurance company or check with your employer's coordinator to find out how you should handle this. Sometimes the parent with the earliest birthdate in the year must submit the children's claims on his or her plan. But that doesn't mean that you will miss out on the higher benefits if your plan covers more than your spouse's. It just means you must go to one plan first. Once you've reached the maximum that plan will cover, you move to the next one to top up the claim to the maximum allowed on the most generous plan. It might take a bit of paperwork and time, but would be well worth it for a large claim.

On the claims form, you must also indicate whether you are covered by any other plan and if you are, you must name the company. This is to avoid double-dipping and fraud. Insurance is intended to reimburse you for money spent, not to provide a gain.

Cover All The Angles

Check out your spouse's and your employee health benefits to make sure you are covered for what you might need. If you don't have access to a health plan through work, you may want to consider an individual private plan.

24. What if I disagree with my insurer on how much I should be reimbursed? Where can I take my complaint?

There are several steps you can take. Start by talking to your insurer, if you disagree with the company's decision. It is possible that the application wasn't clear, that someone made an error, or that second thoughts may make the claim go your way. If that approach doesn't work, you may wish to call the Canadian Life and Health Insurance Association (see "Consumer Resources" in Appendix A for contact information). CLHIA counsellors will listen to your concerns and at least offer their thoughts on whether your complaint is worth pursuing. They may even call the company on your behalf in an attempt to help sort out any misunderstandings. (CLHIA is a trade association representing most life and health insurance companies. It is not a licensing or government body, and has no authority to tell a company what to do.)

In Ontario, each insurance company must have an ombudsperson on staff to handle conflicts. That person may be able to help with disputes outside Ontario as well. Although the ombudsperson position is not a requirement in other parts of Canada, there may be someone on staff at the insurance company who has been designated to handle customer complaints. If you are still not satisfied, go to the provincial government regulatory body (see Appendix A for contact information). In some cases, an ombudsperson or ombudsperson-like position will be set up to assist. Again, however, this office can only use the powers of persuasion, although they are pretty substantial. If you are determined to carry on, your next step would be to take action through the courts.

Checklist

Top 10 questions to ask your insurance provider before you purchase your insurance
1. What does the plan cover? What does it provide that my provincial health care plan doesn't?
2. What does it not cover?
3. Can I choose from among a variety of different coverages?
4. What limitations or conditions apply?
5. Does it cover drugs for a pre-existing condition?
6. Do I need a medical examination?
7. Is there a deductible? If so, how much?
8. How much will my premiums go up for the same coverage as I get older?

When You Have A Claim...
9. How do I make a claim?
10. Can my health care provider bill the insurance company directly? If not, how long does it take for me to be reimbursed?

Keywords

Accidental death and dismemberment	coverage that would provide a lump-sum payment to you or your survivors should an accident result in the loss of a limb, paralysis, or your death.
Deductible	the portion of an insurance claim that you agree to pay out of pocket.
Extended health care	coverage for care and devices beyond what's provided for in your provincial health plan: physical and psychological therapies provided by chiropractors, physiotherapists, speech pathologists, etc.; physical devices such as hearing aids, prosthetic appliances and medical equipment; and home care and nursing.
Health insurance	insurance that will help you pay for medication, as well as vision, dental, or other health care.
Pre-existing condition	an ailment or condition that you have had diagnosed or for which you have seen a physician or are taking treatment before you purchased your insurance policy.
Risk	the possibility of you making a claim.
Underwriter	the company or individual within an insurance company who considers the risk to the company in accepting you as a policyholder.

disability insurance

Government, workplace, and private disability insurance plans

Applying for disability insurance

What happens when you file a disability claim?

Why Disability Insurance?

WHO HASN'T THOUGHT ABOUT LIFE INSURANCE, been approached to buy life insurance, or seen the advertisements for it? Most of us have considered what would happen when we die. Not nearly as many of us have considered what might happen if we were so sick or so seriously injured that we couldn't work. The reality is, more of Canada's working population will become disabled than will die prematurely. The Canadian Life and Health Insurance Association (CLHIA) reports that a 20-year-old man is about three times more likely to be disabled for at least 90 days than he is to die before age 65. A 35-year-old woman is about seven times more likely to face disability than death before age 65.

So why aren't we discussing disability insurance over the back fence the same way we discuss life insurance? We expect to be healthy, and if we are sick, we expect to recover; if we are injured, we expect we could work at something. Not necessarily!

Government programs offer some support for those who become disabled. A short-term disability could make you eligible for benefits under the employment insurance program. A long-term disability could result in benefits under the Canada or Quebec pension plans. If you are working in a designated industry and you are injured on the job, you might have access to benefits through a workers' compensation program. If you are employed in an industry not covered by workers' compensation, you might have access to disability benefits through your company benefits package. If you are working from home, self-employed, or working on contracts, you might have no protection at all. Life and health insurance companies offer disability insurance plans that can be purchased by individuals.

Disability insurance replaces a portion of your income if you become unable, through injury or illness, to work. The snag is, you must have been working for money in the first place, so that eliminates most stay-at-home parents and homemakers. That doesn't mean that those who don't earn money have different financial needs if they become disabled. Just try replacing a caregiver, housekeeper, and cook without spending money. If you fall into this category, you might want to look at critical illness insurance instead. It doesn't cover all illnesses but, because it isn't an income-replacement plan, you don't have to be making money to qualify (see chapter 5).

Different Strokes...

The definition of a disability may vary from one insurance
company to the next. Read it before you buy your policy, so you
will understand any limits on your coverage.

Obtaining disability insurance can be an involved process. You will likely have to answer many questions about your medical and employment history, including details on how much you earn. You will also be asked about investment income assets and liabilities. The insurer will consider all of your income, not just the part you toil for. You may be required to have a medical examination that could include providing blood and urine samples or undergoing other tests.

Getting the package that suits your needs is another consideration. Policies differ on how soon you would collect benefits, and for how long. They also vary in whether disability benefits flow if you can't perform the duties of your own occupation, a job in your field, or any job at all.

As with other types of insurance, ask plenty of questions. Before you make a decision, be sure that you are getting the best option available for your circumstances. It's a very personal product, and a brochure really can't give you an accurate indication of what's available for you.

Frequently Asked Questions ...
About Disability Insurance

1. What is disability insurance?

Disability insurance provides financial benefits to individuals who suffer an accident or illness that leaves them unable to work and earn an income. Workers' compensation plans are a form of disability insurance. The federal government offers disability benefits from the employment insurance program through Employment and Immigration Canada. If you contribute

Your Earning potential

If your earnings increase five percent a year, you will earn this much income between now and age 65.

Age Now	Current Monthly Income (Gross)					
	$2000	$3000	$4000	$5000	$7000	$10,000
25	2,899,195	4,348,792	5,798,389	7,247,986	10,147,181	21,743,960
35	1,594,532	2,391,799	3,189,065	3,986,331	5,580,863	7,972,662
45	793,583	1,190,374	1,587,166	1,983,957	2,777,540	3,967,915
55	301,869	452,804	603,739	754,674	1,056,543	1,509,348

Source: Canadian Life and Health Insurance Association

to the Canada Pension Plan or the Quebec Pension Plan, you may be eligible for disability benefits under these plans. Some employers offer benefit plans that include disability insurance for those who are unable to work on either a short-term or long-term basis. Private disability insurance plans are also available to those who can't access any of the other options, who want a better plan or who want to top up their existing employee benefit plan. All of these plans would help replace part of your income should you become disabled and are no longer able to work.

2. Who needs it?

Anyone who counts on paying bills and daily living expenses from their own income needs disability insurance. An independent construction worker who breaks a leg bike-riding might not be able to earn a living for several months, and may need access to disability benefits. A hairdresser, unable to work through treatment for cancer, would need benefits.

The Canadian Life and Health Insurance Association reports that almost half of all mortgage foreclosures are a result of disabilities. No doubt, most of those people did not expect to find themselves in a position where they could no longer provide for themselves.

You may think that you have enough savings to take care of any emergencies, but savings are soon wiped out if there is no new income to replenish the fund. The CLHIA chart above shows that if you are 25 years old and earning $3,000 a month, your lifetime earnings could surpass $4 million. That's a lot of money to do without. You may have pictured a fatal illness or accident ending your life prematurely and considered the merits of life insurance to care for those left behind. However, CLHIA reports that disability strikes working people far more often than premature death does.

3. Why would I need a private plan?

There are limits to government plans. The workers' compensation programs apply to specific industries, occupations and types of disabilities. If you work in a financial services office, for instance, you aren't likely covered. The pension plan programs apply only if you have paid into them. Likewise for the employment insurance program; not only must you have paid into it, you also have to meet the eligibility requirements for claiming. Self-employed people are excluded. The benefits to these plans are minimal, and wouldn't come close to helping someone who had an above-average income before becoming disabled.

If you opt for a private insurance plan and you become disabled, your disability insurance will be coordinated with all other plans, including worker's compensation or other government programs.

4. Who decides if I am disabled?

When you take out a disability insurance plan, you sign a contract with an insurance provider that outlines what that company would consider a disability. The definition may vary from company to company. Your doctor would have to complete a statement for the company to consider. In addition, the company may look for more information or may ask for another physician to examine you or your file. The contract wording is key.

5. What is considered a disability?

Generally, a disability is an inability to continue to work because of an illness or injury. But, as stated above, the real definition comes in the contract you sign. Read it before you buy the policy to be sure you understand the limits on your policy.

Disability insurance is less clear-cut than other forms of insurance involving health. For example, a back injury for one person may mean

(Almost) Any Job Will Do

Q. You work as a travelling sales representative, and purchase an "any occupation" disability policy. You injure your back in an automobile accident and are no longer able to make sales calls, although you can still work. Can you claim disability benefits?

A. No. "Any occupation" means just that—you must be unable to work in any occupation that is suited to your education, training, and/or experience for your benefits to kick in. If you can work as an inside sales rep, for example, you'll have to do it to earn an income. If you want to receive benefits for being unable to perform any occupation except the one you currently work in, you need to buy an "own occupation" policy. But be prepared to be turned down. Not everyone qualifies for an own occupation policy.

months of bedrest and painkillers; for another person, it may mean a few weeks off work and a few more of soldiering on. Some people may not be able to go back to their regular jobs, while others may not be able to stay home. We react differently to illness and injuries. Just think about how each member of your family copes with a cold. Imagine how differently they would cope with a serious illness.

Insurance companies sell different types of policies that define disability in several ways:

- "Own occupation" policies cover you if you can no longer do the specific job you did before your illness or injury. They are mostly sold as individual insurance policies and are expensive. Professionals, such as doctors, tend to buy them.
- "Regular occupation" policies cover you if you can't do a job within your profession.
- "Any occupation" policies cover you if you couldn't do any job at all.

If you were a chartered accountant, for instance, the "own occupation" policy would kick in if you were no longer able to review financial material for clients; the "regular occupation" policy would pay if you were unable to lecture on accounting; and the "any occupation" policy would apply if you were unable to do any job. That "any job" could be cleaning offices or operating a cash register.

In group policies that you would have through an employee plan, you may have a limit on how long you can claim disability for your own occupation. After a year, you might be expected to accept anything.

If you have a Cadillac plan, you may be able to receive disability benefits because you can't continue working in your own occupation, and at the same time receive payment for working at something else. If the accountant in the above example were to become blind and could no longer perform the usual duties of the profession, he might be able to receive disability benefits and also earn income from the lecture circuit at the same time.

6. Where do I buy it?

You can purchase private disability insurance from a company or representative licensed to sell life and health insurance. If you have life insurance, check with the person who prepared your policy. If you have not developed a relationship with an insurance provider, check with friends and relatives for references. You'll be sharing some very personal information, so you will want to deal with someone you trust and with whom you feel comfortable. If you are starting from scratch, try the Yellow Pages or the Internet, or contact the Canadian Life and Health Insurance Association (see "Consumer Resources" in Appendix A for contact information).

TIP

Read Up!

For a good overview of disability insurance, get the Canadian
Life and Health Insurance Association's free brochure
Disability Insurance: Where Will the Money Come from If
You're Disabled? *Call toll-free 1-800-268-8099 from anywhere*
in Canada (in Toronto: 416-777-2344) to request your copy.

---

7. Can I buy it "off the shelf"?

Group disability insurance that is provided at your workplace is "off the shelf" in that each employee tends to get the same prepared package and there are few, if any, questions asked. Individual disability plans are a different story. You will be asked plenty of questions and, in some cases, you will be required to undergo a medical examination. The individual plans come in three types:

- Noncancellable insurance prevents the policy from being cancelled or the price from changing for the length of the contract.
- Guaranteed renewable insurance requires the insurance company to renew without increasing the premium on an individual basis. Everyone in that class of insurance would have to see the same increase.
- Commercial disability insurance provides more flexibility to the insurance company, which can change the price or decline to renew.

There are different levels of coverage within the above categories that determine when you are disabled (see question 5).

Not all companies offer all products or will make all options available to every applicant. Even group policies may be restricted by the makeup of the organization being insured. Too many claims by your colleagues, coincidental or not, could make the insurer think twice about taking on the risk of insuring your firm.

8. What will I be asked on the application or in the interview?

Typically, the questions start with your insurance representative. That person will fill out an application with you that asks what you do for a living,

---

CAUTION

No Guarantees

If you purchase a commercial disability plan, the insurer can increase the rates on the anniversary of your policy, or even refuse to renew the policy. If you want guaranteed rates and coverage for the duration of your contract, opt for a noncancellable policy.

---

how many hours you work, whether you work away from your home or office, and whether the work is physical. The representative will also want to know about your hobbies and activities outside of work. There will be a number of questions about your current health and your medical history, including past surgeries, and conditions and treatments. You will also be asked about the health of your family members; and whether you smoke, drink alcohol, or use illegal drugs. That application will go to the insurance company for review. The underwriter may want further information or may request a physical examination.

9. Must I undergo a medical?

If the insurance company wants it and you want to proceed with your application for disability insurance, yes, you do. If you are young and healthy, you may not be asked to undergo a medical. The company may send a private nurse or doctor to your home to ask more questions and to carry out a few tests. These tests could include blood, urine and blood pressure tests, a check on your height and weight, and more questions about your medical history. Among other things, the nurse or doctor will be looking for any medical conditions you might have and any evidence of smoking or drug use.

Insurance companies contract out their medical work. The people who come to your home are not employed by the insurer. They will prepare a report that will be sent by their company to the insurance company.

10. May I use my own physician?

If you are uncomfortable about having a stranger carry out an examination or about having an examination conducted in your home, you may ask the insurance company to consider using your own doctor. Since this is not the usual approach, there is no guarantee your request will be granted.

11. Will they tell me if they find something wrong?

The nurse or doctor examining you cannot make a diagnosis on the spot. If they find something unusual, they may suggest you see your family doctor. If lab tests come back with abnormal findings, the company may offer to send your results to your family physician. Your insurance representative will not know the details of your examination. If you have been turned down for insurance, the representative will simply be told that there is a health problem.

12. Are there other restrictions?

Most companies are not interested in applicants who are working fewer than 20 hours a week. They want to insure full-time employees. You may also have difficulty finding disability insurance if you run your own business from your home. It is difficult for the insurer to see if you really do work the hours you say you do. A separate office is a different story. They may do a spot check to ensure you do operate a business. Fraudulent claims cost everyone, and insurers are becoming more active at ferreting them out.

13. Do I have any right to appeal? Can the company just turn me down?

You can always argue a decision. If you are turned down because of a medical test that you think was incorrect, you may retest or go to your family physician for further investigation. Laboratory errors do occur from time to time, and something you've eaten or been exposed to may have affected the outcome of a test. If your family physician re-tests and finds a different result, you may certainly approach the insurance company to reconsider. (See question 26 for more details on how to pursue disputes.)

14. Should I shop around?

Shop around before you formally apply for disability insurance. Companies will want to know if you have been turned down elsewhere. When shopping, ask about the benefits available, the costs of coverage, and how long the benefits will last. If you can get references from others who have had to file claims, it can be very helpful. Price should not be the only consideration. If you do become disabled, having a company that responds quickly and compassionately will be very important.

15. Do companies share files? Will everyone know about my state of health?

Not everyone shares files, but your medical history may be sent to an organization called the Medical Information Bureau (MIB). When you sign your application for insurance you may also be authorizing the company to share some information. MIB is neither an insurance company nor a government office. The organization describes itself as a "membership association" of life and health insurance companies set up to stop fraud. If you have a significant health condition, your insurance company will send a coded report to MIB. If you apply for insurance through another company, and it checks with MIB, your report will come up and can be compared with what you told the insurer on your application. The files are kept for seven years. If you are curious or concerned, you can check with MIB to see if a file exists for you. If it does, you may request to see it. (See "Consumer Resources" in Appendix A for contact information.)

You will likely be asked on your application if you have ever been refused insurance. Previous refusal is a clue to insurers to ask more questions, but it doesn't mean that you won't be allowed insurance at the second company. One firm may have different restrictions than the other.

16. If I say I am a non-smoker but I do take a cigarette from time to time, will the company find out? Will it cancel the policy?

It might find out. And if it does, yes, it might cancel the policy. If you file a claim and investigations show your activities are different from what you presented at the interview, the company may have grounds to deny your claim. All insurers take fraud seriously and have decreasing tolerance for even the "little white lies." So don't hide the wine bottles and the ashtrays to get the coverage. Even if the insurance company doesn't do a thorough check on your lifestyle before you are insured, you can be sure all the details will be covered—or uncovered—if you file a claim.

17. How much does disability insurance cost?

For individual policies, the price varies widely based on your age, gender, occupation, lifestyle habits, like smoking, and, of course, the type of policy you buy (see question 5). A 40-year-old male construction worker who doesn't smoke, for instance, could pay about $100 a month for a policy that would provide him with $2,000 a month in benefits if he were to become disabled. A 40-year-old male chartered accountant who doesn't smoke could pay $63 a month for a policy that would provide $2,000 a month in benefits. Even though it costs less, the accountant's policy would be much more enhanced, including benefits until he's 65 without asking him to take any occupation if he were disabled and could no longer work as an accountant. The difference lies in the kind of work each individual does. The chartered accountant's work is less risky to his health than the construction worker's.

The Claims Scenario

18. When can I file a claim?

If you have an injury or illness that stops you from working for an extended period of time, you may file a claim. Check your policy on when disability insurance payments begin. Each plan is different and there are variances in waiting periods. You may hear your insurance company call them "elimination periods." You might expect to recover from your ailment in a matter of weeks and don't think it's worth claiming. In the end, it might not be, but you never know how your health will turn. Suppose you injure your back and take a few days off work. You head back two days later assuming you are on the mend. A few months later the problem may return requiring another two days off. If the problem is recurrent and at the end of a few years you've had 30 days off for the same injury, you may have satisfied the waiting period and be eligible for benefits if the ailment keeps you out of the workforce again. Keep records and check with your insurance company to see if they want copies of them as your absences from work occur.

Don't wait to file your claim. Missing 30, 60 or 90 days of income to

TIP

Keep It Handy

Make sure all of your insurance documents are well labelled and easy to find. If you are seriously ill or injured, a family member or friend may need access to them to start your claim for you.

qualify may be hard enough without having to wait another month before the cheques start arriving.

19. How quickly will the cheques arrive, and for how long?

It depends on what kind of policy you have purchased and on the waiting period. You may have opted for a plan that kicks in after 90 days of disability, or longer. Your premium may be slightly lower if you've opted for a longer waiting period. It's similar to the deductibles you find in property and health insurance policies (see chapters 2 and 5). Put in your claim promptly. If everything checks out medically, you will continue to receive cheques in the amount agreed to in your policy for the length of time agreed to in your policy; it could be several years or until you are 65. If you have an ongoing disability, you will likely need further medical assessments. The insurer will not want to keep you on the payroll without confirming that you are still unable to work. With some policies, you may be able to collect off the top if you are unable to work in your old job, but will eventually lose benefits unless you are unable to work in any job. You will need a statement from your physician almost immediately. Further information may be required, or you may be asked to see another doctor for an independent assessment.

20. Is the money I receive mine to spend as I see fit, or must I have spending approved?

The money you receive through disability benefits is to replace your income. It has no strings attached. You may also be receiving health insurance benefits that will pay for specific products and services. For those benefits, you would require receipts and approvals. The disability benefit can be spent as you wish.

21. How much money will I get?

That depends on the policy you have. You could be covered for up to two-thirds of your gross salary. It is very unlikely that you will ever see 100 per cent of your income covered, so don't think that you can live as well as you did before. All of the coverage to which you have access will be considered

Playing The Waiting Game

Q. You want to buy disability insurance, but you find the premiums too high. Is there any way you can reduce the cost without skimping on the coverage you need?
A. Consider extending the waiting period for benefits to kick in. The longer you wait, the less you pay. Compare the premiums for 30-, 90-, and 180-day waiting periods. But before opting for a longer waiting period, make sure you have enough money set aside that you could get by for, say, six months without an income.

in your claim. Government plans, auto insurance (see chapter 3), or other programs that replace your income will be included in the calculation to bring you to the maximum payable. In addition, you may have many other expenses related to your treatment that will cut into your daily living funds.

When you applied for disability insurance, your unearned income was also taken into consideration. Interest you receive from investments, for instance, may result in your receiving lower insurance benefits than someone in a similar situation with no investments to draw on. That should have been made clear when you first signed up.

22. Am I free to travel while on disability?

You are not required to stay at home while receiving disability benefits. That said, if you are unable to lift boxes, but head south for months of golfing, eyebrows may be raised.

23. Does it matter whether it is a physical or mental disability?

No. Each illness is judged on its own merits. Disability benefits for people suffering from severe stress, for instance, have become more common. If a doctor has confirmed that you are unable to work because of your illness, you will receive benefits.

Calculate Where You Stand

A. What You Need

Add up your cost of living and see how far you're willing to cut back. In the first column, list your current monthly expenses. (For annual expenses, such as insurance and vacation, divide by 12.) Then, list your expenses if you became disabled. If you spend a lot for clothes, commuting and lunch, you might think your expenses would fall if you can't work. Maybe not. You may need special care, equipment or even home renovations.

Expenses	Today	If Disabled
Housing:		
▓ mortgage or rent	_____	_____
▓ property tax	_____	_____
▓ utilities	_____	_____
▓ insurance	_____	_____
▓ maintenance & repair	_____	_____
Food:	_____	_____
Transportation:		
▓ public transit	_____	_____
▓ car loan or lease	_____	_____
▓ car insurance & license	_____	_____
▓ gas, parking, & maintenance	_____	_____
Clothing:	_____	_____
Health care:		
▓ services & products	_____	_____
▓ insurance	_____	_____
Financial security:		
▓ life insurance	_____	_____
▓ RRSPs	_____	_____
▓ regular savings	_____	_____
▓ special savings	_____	_____
Education:	_____	_____
Recreation & vacations:	_____	_____
Other: (include spending money, debts, business & tax obligations)	_____	_____
Total Monthly Expenses:	_____	_____

B. What You Have

What sources of income could you draw on in the event of a disability? List your current coverage. (Be aware that when more than one plan applies, benefits are usually integrated and capped at 85 percent or less of normal earnings.)

	Are You Covered?	Monthly Benefit (if known)
Government:		
▓ Workers' Compensation	_____	_____
▓ Unemployment Insurance	_____	_____
▓ CPP	_____	_____
Group:		
▓ sick leave	_____	_____
▓ short term (weekly indemnity)	_____	_____
▓ long term	_____	_____
Individual:	_____	_____
Special Purpose:		
▓ to cover loans	_____	_____
▓ to cover mortgage	_____	_____
▓ to cover business overhead	_____	_____
▓ other	_____	_____

24. Are my premiums tax deductible?

The 1998 federal budget allowed self-employed people to deduct premiums for health and dental insurance. It's a bit different with disability insurance because you would be receiving an income as the benefit. Disability insurance premiums are not tax deductible if the benefits are intended to be tax-free. If you become disabled, you probably wouldn't want to give up part of your benefits to income tax, so you might be better off not using it as a deduction now to protect the full amount later.

C. Is There Other Money You Could Draw on?

Source	Amount Available	Considerations
Spousal Income: (if applicable)	_____	
Emergency savings:	_____	If you saved five percent of your earnings each year, six months of disability could wipe out ten years of savings.
Investments:	_____	Are they locked in? Could you get a fair market price?
RRSPs:	_____	Tax will be deducted at source. Amounts withdrawn cannot be replaced.
Borrow against home:	_____	May be hard to do and would strain cash flow.
Borrow against life insurance:	_____	Reduces death benefit.

The Bottom Line

Total monthly income available (B+C): _____

Minus total monthly expenses (A): _____

Where You Stand: _____

Source: Canadian Life and Health Insurance Association

25. If I am well enough to go back to work for a while and then take ill again, am I still eligible for benefits?

This is an important question to ask when you are purchasing a disability plan. Plans differ on the waiting period required before claiming a second time if you have a relapse. It is usually shorter than the first.

26. What happens if I am able to work part-time? Will I receive partial benefits?

Your insurance company will be anxious to get you back to work in any capacity. If you are prepared to go back part-time, they may arrange to continue paying part of your benefits. You may not be able to do your old job, but you may be interested in trying something completely different. You may be able to negotiate another arrangement or a lump-sum payment to help you move on. The insurance company doesn't want you on disability for the rest of your life if you don't need to be. If you can work at something, both sides win. The company won't have to continue payments forever, and you will gain from getting back into activities.

27. Will I be subject to more physical examinations by doctors and nurses other than my own?

You might be. Diagnosing a disability can be trickier and more subjective than diagnosing an illness. Two people could be diagnosed with similar cancers. Medical tests could show the presence of antibodies or tumours that make it easy to label. But deciding how much work each of those people can continue to do is a different story. One individual may be emotionally devastated, exhausted by treatments, and unable to manage the pain; the other may have a different threshold and be happier working as long as possible. The insurer may want a second opinion on the degree of disability for the individual involved.

28. Do I have the right to appeal if the insurance company cuts me off?

Yes, ask the company to send in writing to your doctor its medical reasons for cutting you off or turning you down in the first place. Talk to your doctor about it, since some of the language may not mean anything to those of us without medical school training. If you still think the reasons are unfair, call the Canadian Life and Health Insurance Association's Consumer Assistance Centre. Counsellors there may be able to work with you and the insurer to sort out any misunderstandings. (CLHIA is a trade association representing insurance companies and has no authority over those companies.) If you still have concerns, call the company ombudsperson or your provincial regulatory agency (see "Consumer Resources" in Appendix A for contact information). The last resort is court action.

Checklist

Top 10 questions to ask your insurance provider before you purchase your disability insurance.

1. How does the insurance company define a disability in the policy?
2. What kind of coverage is it—"own occupation," "regular occupation," or "any occupation?" What is the difference in cost for each?
3. What type of insurance is it—noncancellable, guaranteed renewable, or commercial disability?
4. How long are any benefits payable?
5. How much of my current salary will the policy pay? Are the benefits indexed to inflation?
6. Are there any limitations or restrictions on the policy that I should be aware of?
7. What is the waiting period before I can claim benefits? How much money can I save on my premiums by extending the waiting period?
8. If I go back to work and then suffer a relapse, what is the waiting period before I can claim benefits again?
9. If I am able to work part-time, can I receive partial benefits? Is the waiting period any different than for full benefits? Are there any restrictions?
10. Can I increase my coverage at any time? Do I need another medical examination to do so?

Keywords

Benefits   the payment you would receive through your insurance plan if you become disabled.

Disability   the inability, due to illness or injury, to continue working.

Pre-existing condition   an ailment or condition that you have had diagnosed or for which you have seen a physician or are taking treatment before you purchased your insurance policy.

Underwriter   the company or individual within an insurance company who considers the risk to the company in accepting you as a policyholder.

travel insurance

Insurance for emergency health care while you are on holidays

Health care insurance for students studying abroad

Cancellation insurance

Baggage insurance

What happens when you file an emergency health
insurance claim

Why travel insurance?

A H, HOLIDAYS. Think of the choices you have to dream about: sun, sea, and warmth; theatre, nightclubs, and fine dining; galleries, museums, and the opera; skiing, hiking, and cozy cabins; food poisoning, broken bones, and lost luggage?!!! Wait a minute, that's not what we had planned. Of course not, but if you do fall ill on vacation, particularly away from your home country, you'll be better off knowing that you thought about it in advance and have a contingency plan.

After scrimping and saving all year for the dream vacation, you may have little interest in surrendering even more money for insurance which you certainly don't expect to use. Only the pessimists among us would expect to get sick on vacation. But you should at least have thought about the possibility before you go away. Play the "what if" game. What if you broke a leg skiing and couldn't drive your family home from the chalet you had rented for the holidays? What if your honeymoon began with food poisoning from one of the many buffets you couldn't pass up? What if you had a heart attack or stroke while on holiday? Could you pay thousands of dollars a day for hospital care in Florida? Would you have someone available who could manage the arrangements? Could you pay for the care you needed immediately? Would you understand the language of local medical authorities?

You've seen the ads for travel insurance. They're hard to miss. "One quick call, one worry-free vacation," one of them says. Well, not so fast. The person selling the insurance may want it to be a quick call, and you may feel the same way, but it shouldn't be. Take the time to find out what you are buying and make sure you are speaking to someone who knows the product. Remember, travel insurance is a product and, like the warranty on your VCR, you should know what is and isn't covered should something go wrong.

Insurance is a business, and no company will want to insure someone who is very likely to file a claim. That costs money instead of making it. If you are young and healthy, you're all set. If you are aging and burdened with medical problems, it's a different story. However, there is a big difference between applying for travel health insurance and applying for regular health insurance or life insurance. You will not have to undergo a medical examination before you are approved. You also won't likely have to answer extensive questions about your medical history. In many cases, you may just have to fill out a brief application that asks for your name, address, health card number, and how long you are planning to travel. You send in a cheque, and the application is either accepted or not.

If your application is accepted, a real policy arrives that outlines what *isn't* covered. If you don't read it, you may not know what risks you are taking on until you have a medical emergency. The biggest restriction will be for what insurers call "pre-existing conditions." If you've been treated for a medical problem in the nine months or so before your trip and that condition acts up on your holiday, it won't be covered. Don't think that because you haven't been asked specifically about a particular disease that it will be covered. The exclusion is broad. If you do have a claim, your family physician will likely be consulted, so there's no point in trying to hide the truth. If you are concerned about the details and don't want to risk travelling without coverage for your troubles, check with the insurer first. You may find that, while funding for care for a heart attack may be out of the question, treatment for a broken leg suffered on the golf course would be covered. If the insurer has asked and you have failed to disclose your true medical condition, you may find nothing is covered. Didn't mention that heart problem? Forget about having your broken leg repaired on the insurance company's tab. Minor health issues shouldn't be a problem. If in doubt, ask your insurance provider.

Insurers might also balk at paying for expenses related to risky activities, such as hang-gliding or mountain climbing. So read your policy before you set out to scale that peak in Nepal. They also may not cover you if your illness or injury develops in a war zone. Again, check before you make your arrangements, so you can at least assess your own risks.

For those who fear losing all the hard-earned money they've poured into their vacation before they've even left the house, there is also cancellation insurance. It won't protect you if you've simply had a change of heart, but can protect your holiday investment from a medical problem that leaves you unable to travel. Some plans may cover your travel expenses if a meeting is called off or your travelling companion is unwell.

Even if you make it to your holiday destination, your luggage may not. Baggage insurance can help replace lost, stolen, or damaged luggage. You may win some compensation from your airline if the goods have

disappeared in transit, but the amounts may not be as high or cover as
many variables as baggage insurance. It's just one more thing to consider
before you head off for what should now be a worry-free vacation.

Frequently Asked Questions ...
About Travel Insurance

Travel health insurance

1. Why do I need travel health insurance?

Remember the last time you bought new medical supplies for your travel
bag? Bandages, antiseptic ointment, analgesics, tweezers, alcohol swabs,
thermometer, sunburn relief, anti-diarrhea pills, laxatives—it didn't take a
very big toiletry bag to absorb $100 worth of drugstore goods, did it? Now
imagine how much it would cost if you became seriously ill on holiday and
needed help beyond what fit in your suitcase.

Health care is expensive and often exceeds the savings most of us have
stored up for vacation. No matter how cautious we are, accidents and illnesses do happen. One round of food poisoning could quickly see you rack
up a bill of thousands of dollars a day for hospital care. If you'd rather
spend those thousands on your next vacation, you may want to consider
spending the tens of dollars travel health insurance would cost instead.

2. What does travel health insurance cover?

Depending on the package you purchase, travel health insurance might offer benefits for emergency hospital or other medical services, prescription drugs, X-rays and lab fees, ambulance services, private nursing or wheel-chairs. Caught a ball at spring training? Your travel health insurance would probably pay for emergency dental care too.

If you have to get back to Canada for immediate medical treatment, your insurance plan might pay for a plane ticket on a regular flight with a med-ical attendant accompanying you. If you can't travel on a regular flight, an emergency air ambulance flight might be included with a doctor and nurse on board. Your coverage may also get a relative to your bedside, or get your vehicle back home. In the event of a fatal injury or illness, your travel insur-ance would pay to send your body home. You can't simply request those benefits, however. Access to them usually depends on a medical opinion on your condition. Your insurer wants to make sure you really need the service and that it would be safe for you before authorizing payment. Unfortunately, the fraudsters among us have made it necessary to require some checks in the system.

3. Doesn't my government plan cover all of my needs?

We hear a lot of talk about Canada's health care system, particularly in rela-tion to the system in the United States. Most of our health care is paid for through our tax dollars. A large pool of money ensures that we have access to the care we might need, whether we are likely to need it or not. You see a

TIP

Visit Your Pharmacist

Get your prescriptions filled before you go away, and make sure you have enough to last you for the length of your holiday plus a few days.

doctor and no bill arrives, no money changes hands. Provincial health care plans cover most of your needs at home. However, those public insurance programs are based on Canadian costs. Health care costs may be higher in the country you are visiting. In the United States, for instance, there is less reliance on the tax system to fund health care and a much greater private involvement. That has an effect on the cost of services.

If you have a health problem when you are away, your government plan will pay only what the Canadian costs would be, not the real costs in the country you are visiting. For instance, provincial plans would cover from between $75 and $800 a day for a hospital stay. But the charge in an American hospital could be several thousands of dollars a day, as high as $10,000 a day for intensive care! Physicians' fees tend to be higher in the U.S. as well, something we don't usually have to consider at home. Our provincial plans will cover from about $50 to $100 for each visit to a physician. American fees are well beyond that. So, although your government plan would cover some of your expenses, it wouldn't cover everything.

Don't count on advice from your cousins in the next province, by the way. Each provincial plan is different; an allowable expense under British Columbia's plan, for instance, may not be covered under Newfoundland's plan. Recognizing their own limits, the provincial health ministries themselves recommend you purchase extra insurance when you leave the country.

CAUTION

You Ain't Necessarily Covered

Just because the insurance company doesn't ask you a lot of questions on the application form (unlike an application for life insurance), don't assume you are automatically covered if you have a claim. Check the exclusions (what isn't covered) and the definition of "pre-existing condition" so you don't get a nasty surprise at claims time.

Credit Cards May Have Their Limits

Don't assume that the travel medical insurance that may be offered with some credit cards will provide you with the same coverage as a separate travel health plan. Check for any restrictions and limitations, and compare the coverage with that of a separate plan.

4. Don't the new full-service gold credit cards cover everything?

They would have you believe that, but guess what? Some restrictions apply. It's tough to sort out just what you are covered for with all the special deals, offers, and new services we are supposed to be getting from credit cards, memberships, and other programs. The key, as always, is to check it out before you count on it. With the credit card offers, you may have to book all your travel and accommodations on that card to have it take effect. You may also be limited by how long your trip lasts. If you do consider leaving everything up to the plastic, you may also want to know who underwrites the insurance business of the credit card. It's likely that a large insurance company is the underwriter, which may help you assess your level of comfort with the expected service should you have a claim. Compare the coverages available through the card with those that are offered through a separate travel health insurance package.

5. What if I'm just visiting my family in the next province?

An agreement among all the provinces and territories is in place so that your health needs can be met wherever you are in Canada. Since Quebec's participation in the agreement is limited, Quebec residents should check with the province on specifics. Carry your health card with you at all times. The medical staff caring for you while you are on holiday must be able to confirm that you are covered by the insurance plan in your own province.

That said, although your care by physicians, nurses, and other medical staff would be dealt with without you having to open your wallet, the plans may not cover any extras to get you home as fast and as comfortably as you might like. If you had an attack of appendicitis while you were on a cross-country cycling tour, your government plan would take care of your surgery and treatment but might not cover the costs of an ambulance or a flight home. You might also want a family member brought to your bedside. If it's not included in government plans, private insurance might cover the costs.

If you are attending college or university in another province, notify your provincial health plan officials in advance. They will want to know where you are studying and when you plan to return. You may have to renotify them each year you are away to ensure your home province plan will continue to cover you.

As with most types of insurance, we tend not to think about health insurance until we need it. Before you go away, check out what is and is not covered by the government plan. In fact, it might help to speak to provincial health insurance staffers who know about health insurance but are not trying to sell it.

6. What happens when I'm travelling on business?

Your company insurance plan may cover you as an employee, but ask first. You might not expect that to be a problem in a large company where a lot of travel is required, but don't assume anything. Your company might also make assumptions about what arrangements you routinely make. Perhaps it had always been left to your administrative assistant to sort out the details and he's on holiday. Maybe the previous person in your position preferred to make her own arrangements. If you are covered by a company plan, that plan may cover what they think you need rather than what you want. Be sure you know what your coverage entails before you go.

If you are posted in a foreign office for an extended time, make sure you have checked with your provincial health insurance program to be certain that you won't lose your status and access to government health care benefits. If you will be away for longer than the number of months or days allowed by your provincial plan, you may be able to get special permission to have the coverage extended. Private insurance plans usually stipulate that

Keep Your Home Health Insurance In Place

If you plan to be out of the country for an extended period of time, make sure your provincial health plan will remain in effect. Ask health officials how long you can be away without losing access to government health insurance. Remember, if you lose the government health insurance, you also lose the private travel health insurance.

you must be covered by a provincial plan to be eligible. If you lose your provincial health plan status, you lose your private coverage too. Check the calendar and rules closely.

If you travel with a companion or take along a family member on your frequent-flyer points, you may need extra coverage. They wouldn't likely be included in an employee plan.

7. Do students studying abroad need additional health insurance?

Yes, but a student isn't really a vacationer, despite what we might remember of our school days! Be careful. You might think that learning Spanish in Spain is a holiday but, in fact, you will be a student, not a vacationer. Vacationers purchase travel health insurance that is to be used for emergencies only. Let's say an emergency does come up for our student of Spanish. The insurance company will work to make certain that the patient's immediate needs are met and her condition is stabilized so she can be brought back to Canada for further treatment. The airline ticket is one-way. That student should have insurance that covers far more than emergencies. She might need regular dental treatments, repeat prescriptions for a simple condition, access to a physician for bad colds and flus. If a medical procedure were needed, she wouldn't likely want to interrupt her studies to come back to Canada when the work could be done in Spain. If she did come home, she'd be paying for the flight back to Spain to complete her studies.

Lessons #1: Find Insurance!

Q. You decide to spend a year studying ancient history in Greece.
Can you be covered by travel health insurance?
A. No, not a good idea. Travel health insurance that you
purchase in Canada covers you for emergency treatment only,
with the aim of returning you to Canada, and the Canadian
health care system, as soon as possible. You won't want to
interrupt your studies to fly back to Canada for, say, a broken leg
or an aching tooth (and then pay for your flight back to Greece
again). You need to buy health insurance from a provider
in Greece before you leave Canada.

Instead of buying travel health insurance, look for a company licensed to sell insurance in the country being made a temporary home. Do this before you leave Canada. You don't want to find yourself sick on the first day of classes with no way to pay for a doctor's care because you haven't found an insurer yet. Ask the larger Canadian firms if they have a link to companies in the country of studies. Failing that, try the embassy, the school you will be attending, or the Internet.

A reminder to students studying within Canada, but away from their home province: talk to officials at your home provincial health plan before you go to ensure your government coverage continues for the full length of your studies.

8. Would relatives on an extended visit to Canada need extra coverage?

Yes, but don't expect your plan (government or private) to extend to them, even though they are your relatives. Arrange for insurance well before your family arrives to make certain there is no lag. If you wait until they get to Canada and their first experience with icy pathways and heavy luggage results in a broken leg, you'll be on the hook for care. Remember that an insurance policy covers you for what *might* happen, not for what already has. Some companies offer very specific plans for visitors to Canada. For some options on who to call, consult the Yellow Pages.

If your relatives are immigrating to Canada, there is insurance available to bridge them until they qualify for a provincial health card.

9. Does it matter where I'm travelling?

If you are staying in Canada and just visiting another province, your needs wouldn't likely be as great. An agreement among the provinces ensures that your health needs are met no matter where you are in Canada (see question 5). But the provincial plans are not identical. Some will pay for ambulance services, for instance, while others will not. If you want to be sure that you have all the bases covered, you may wish to buy additional insurance. If you skip extra insurance, you accept the risk of having to pay for some services you might need (insurers call it "self-insuring"). So if you do become ill on an out-of-province visit, don't forget to ask about costs before accepting or requesting any services.

Outside of Canada, there are other factors that may determine your financial risk threshold. What kind of health care do they have in the country you are visiting? Is it a socialized system or private system? What are the costs of hospital stays, physician consultations, casts, bandages, and medications? Because France has a socialized health care system similar to Canada's, the costs there might be more consistent with ours. Therefore, if

CAUTION

It's Not All In The Family

Relatives visiting from another country will not be covered by your government medical insurance, even if they are members of your extended family. You can arrange for private health coverage for them, but do it before they land in Canada, just in case.

your provincial plan covers foreign costs that roughly match Canada's, you may not be out of pocket for as much as you would be in the United States with its private system. On the other hand, studying the health care plans of all the nations you will visit on your world tour is a bit excessive. Wouldn't you rather be studying the maps? If in doubt, buy extra coverage.

If you are visiting a small emerging nation, there might not be the standard of care you would expect at home. No amount of money can buy services and supplies that simply don't exist. In that case, you would want to consider whether you could buy adequate additional insurance to get you as quickly and safely as possible to a nation that could meet your needs at close to Canadian standards. Some adventure travellers carry many of their own medical supplies, such as sterile syringes, needles, and medications to ensure that local shortages don't affect their personal care.

Some insurance plans do not provide coverage in all parts of the world. Again, check with your insurance provider before embarking on that round-the-world adventure tour.

10. Is spending six months in the sunny south in a second home considered travelling?

Yes. Make sure you have insurance that will cover you at your home away from home. If you are a snowbird, you should buy packages designed for people in your particular circumstances. However, you will likely find that once you hit age 65, the rates change. Second, you may find that you can purchase insurance on an annual basis designed for folks who spend considerable periods of time away from their home base. If it doesn't save you money, it should at least save you time, because you won't have to be reapplying every time you head south. You may also find discounts for using the same insurance company without filing a claim.

As is the case with business travellers (see question 6), check with your provincial insurance plan to find out how long you are permitted to be away before you lose access to government health insurance. Remember, if you lose the government health insurance, you also lose the private travel health insurance. Some travellers interrupt their time in the sun and head back over the border for just a few days to ensure that their lengthy trip is counted as two visits instead of one.

Most snowbirds count on travel health insurance to get them through, but it is very important to remember that travel insurance is designed for emergencies. If you have a mishap, your insurer will pay for your immediate treatment until you are well enough to travel home for any further help you need. No matter how comfortable it may be, you can't stay on the beach waiting for your follow-up care. If you really wanted those needs cared for without having to face the ice and snow again, you would have to purchase a full health insurance package designed for the American system. The costs could be prohibitive.

If you are a gambler and think you can do without any of this, it may interest you to know that the average cost of moving a patient from Florida to Toronto is $13,000. That wouldn't include the cost of a hospital stay down there first!

11. Where do I buy travel insurance?

If you've used a travel agent to book your trip, you may have been offered insurance at that time. Travel agencies generally have a selection of brochures that include applications for insurance, and often, you can purchase it through the agent. You may also have some coverage through your credit cards, requiring no separate policy purchase, but be careful of restrictions (see question 4). Applications for travel insurance may also be available through your bank, and payment may be accepted there as well. Your home, car, or life insurance agent or broker may be able to offer you travel insurance, or you could go directly to a company specializing in travel insurance. Many clubs, professional associations, alumni groups, and other organizations also offer travel insurance. Check the Yellow Pages or call the Canadian Life and Health Insurance Association's Information Centre for listings (see "Consumer Resources" in Appendix A for contact information).

Don't expect a bank teller or travel agent to know all the ins and outs of insurance. That's not their area of expertise. Call the insurance company or use an insurance representative for detailed help.

12. Should I shop around or accept what the travel agent offers?

At the very least, carefully examine what you have been offered. Make sure you are getting access to services you might need or want if you are sick or

Look At A Yearly Plan

If you are a frequent traveller, look into an annual plan that will cover you for the whole year, rather than purchasing insurance every time you leave the country. This is especially good for those who live near the Canada–U.S. border.

injured. By all means, shop around if you have the time. Some companies offer discounts for certain customers who have used their service before without filing a claim, while some have special packages for frequent travellers. If you are a snowbird, for instance, and travel every year, you may find special loyalty rates. If you live close to the Canada–U.S. border and make frequent shopping trips stateside, look for companies that offer coverage on a yearly basis. That way, you won't have to buy a policy every time you crave Buffalo wings or Seattle's best bargains.

Caution: Be sure to check the exclusions—what is *not* covered—in the particular policy you are planning to buy, as well as any limitations in the coverage.

13. How much do I have to tell them before I purchase?

Everything they ask. For this particular type of insurance, however, insurers often don't ask much. The application forms look for basic information about birth dates, provincial health insurance numbers, and dates of departures and returns. The big "if" in your coverage comes from the line that says: "We do not cover expenses for any problems related to a pre-existing condition." Unlike with life insurance, you won't have had a physical examination before buying this product. So any arguments about what is and isn't covered will come after the fact, unless you have made a special effort to find out in advance what conditions that particular company considers "pre-existing." The pamphlets don't offer many examples and conditions to work with. You must call the insurance provider to really be sure.

14. Does travel health insurance cover everything?

Not by a long shot. Insurance is designed to cover unforeseen emergencies, not the costs of what has a good chance of happening. So if you are eight months pregnant and head to California to put your feet up in the sun for the last time, you would pay the costs of delivery if your baby is born early. The insurance industry calls that a pre-existing condition. In other words, you know you are pregnant and you can expect to give birth requiring medical care. That and other pre-existing conditions are the source of many disputes between travellers and insurers. You may think that you are in "good condition" because you are on anti-hypertensive medication. Your insurer might argue that you have a "pre-existing condition" and will not cover costs incurred if you have a heart attack on holiday. So that you are clear on what's covered, you may want to tell the insurer what medications you are on and what treatments you have had recently. You'll be able to get an indication up front as to whether problems arising from those health concerns would be covered if you have a flare-up. The specific condition may be excluded from coverage, but you may be able to get everything else included. Check it out before you purchase.

Each company sets its own definition of pre-existing conditions. Some will cover certain conditions if they have been stable for three months. For

SCENARIO

Get To The Heart Of The Matter

Q. Six months ago, you were treated for a heart condition that has now stabilized. Do you have to tell your travel insurer?
A. Yes. Don't take a chance on having your condition flare up while you are away, only to find out you have no coverage for it. If you hadn't told your insurer about your condition beforehand, that would give the company a perfect excuse to deny your claim—and don't think it won't take that opportunity! Discuss any treatments you have had and medications you are taking with your insurer before you leave, to see if you will be covered.

others or for other conditions, six, or even nine, months may be the benchmark. Insurers will be looking for any deterioration of your condition, new or more severe symptoms of that condition, or a change of medication for that condition in the time period set out in the policy. Cardiac and lung conditions are of particular concern and may be noted specifically in the policy.

Insurers are also not keen on covering risky activities. If you are very active, you may not see much risk in scuba diving, bungee jumping, or hang-gliding. Your insurer may see it differently. If you plan to soar from great heights or plunge to the depths of the ocean, at least find out if treatment for broken bones from such adventures would be covered. In fact, injuries or illnesses resulting from most adventure activities are usually not covered. Similarly, if you head into a war zone, you may not be covered for any injuries caused by the war. With some companies, you may not be covered at all if you travel to a war zone. Suicide is never covered.

You may not be asked specifically about any of these conditions or activities before you buy insurance. Read the literature and the policy to know what is and isn't covered. It may change your holiday activities.

15. What will travel health insurance cost?

Cost depends on how long your trip lasts and how old you are. The older you are, the higher the price. Insurers base their premiums on the likelihood

---

SCENARIO

Don't Climb Every Mountain (unless you're insured!)

Q. You are about to embark on an adventure tour that includes a trek in the Himalayas. Will your travel medical plan cover you if you injure yourself along the way?

A. It depends on the plan. Many travel medical plans exclude (do not cover) certain sporting activities like mountain climbing. Check before you trek.

---

of people in your age group having a medical problem on holiday. You may be a healthier, more active 60-year-old than your 25-year-old couch-potato neighbour, but the rates are based on group, not individual, experiences. A 60-year-old could expect to pay about $35 for a two-week trip. The 25-year-old neighbour would pay about $30 for the same trip. That would buy them benefits of up to $1 million. For longer stays, the premiums increase. If you are a frequent traveller and wish to purchase once for the whole year, annual plans might be available for about $60 a year for those under 55 years of age, and for more than $100 a year for those over 55. If you are older than 65, the price jumps to the $200 range. If you are past 70, you may not be able to get travel health insurance from all companies.

What you get for your money will appear to be the same in the brochures, but based on your medical history, you will find variances if you file a claim. If you've been treated for a heart condition in the past months (with some companies it could be up to nine months), treatment for a heart attack will not be covered. If you have never had any hint of heart trouble but have a heart attack on holiday, your treatment will be covered.

If you already have coverage through an individual health insurance plan, travel insurance may be included or may be purchased for a lower price with higher benefits.

The Claims Scenario

16. Can I arrange to have treatments at my sunny winter retreat? It would be a great place to recuperate.

It certainly would be nice to recover from illness while gazing at the ocean, especially if the bug you caught wasn't too terrible. Unfortunately, that's not what travel insurance is for. Travel insurance is designed for emergency care only, not long-term care. If you are ill, once you are well enough to travel, every effort will be made to get you back home for longer-term treatment or other procedures. Try not to think of travel insurance as a replacement for your provincial government plan; think of it as a bridge to get you well enough to return to Canadian care.

17. My insurer says I have to come home, but the doctors who cared for me on holiday say I should have surgery first. Who's right?

Watch out for the squeeze play. Both "teams" are looking out for your best interests and their own. As we discussed in question 16, your insurance policy is to cover costs that will stabilize you so that you can travel home. You may have had a heart attack in the community with the best heart surgeon in the world, but unless travelling will jeopardize your health or you can't continue without immediate surgery, you are going home. That may be hard to take when you have built a relationship with the team that helped you through your trauma. Keep in mind, though, that there is a different business component to some health care systems where it might be in the providers' best interests to have a well-insured customer/patient stay for further tests and procedures.

There are checks and balances in the system, and your care will be well scrutinized because of your two "teams." Before you are moved, a physician in the country you are visiting will have to agree to release you. If it isn't safe to move you, that release won't be signed. At the same time, a physician in Canada must agree to accept you. Again, if that doctor doesn't believe it would be safe to move you or if there is no hospital to accept you, you won't be moved.

Your insurer and its medical contacts will be basing their decisions on the Canadian standard of care. Another country may have different standards. For instance, a two-month wait for hip-replacement surgery may be acceptable here, but unusually long or short in another country. You are from Canada, your insurance was purchased in Canada, and you are covered by Canadian government insurance plans. Your care will be based on Canadian standards.

18. Whom do I trust?

Both sides are working to take care of you. If the advice you receive conflicts or seems different from your past experience, call your family physician. Your doctor will have the best picture of your medical history and may be able to help you understand your condition and put it in context with that history. Your insurer may contact your family doctor in any case, as your claim is processed.

19. If I get sick, will the bill be sent directly to the insurance company?

In some countries (particularly in the United States), the hospital will bill your provincial health plan and your insurance company directly. The provincial plan usually pays first, with the private plan picking up services that are not covered by the government. Any doctor you see outside of a hospital may prefer a different arrangement. If so, you may have to pay up front and submit your bills to be reimbursed later. Some companies won't pay for anything if you haven't let them know that you are accepting medical care out of the country. But there is usually a short grace period. No one expects you to call your insurer before an ambulance if you are having a heart attack.

Your insurer will pick up the usual costs of each item. If you've landed in the Ritz of hospitals and everything from bandages to rooms costs 10 per cent more than elsewhere, you will be responsible for the balance. Insurers call it "balance billing." Ask when you buy your policy if your insurer does balance bill. If so, and you have a choice where you are hospitalized, you may want to keep that in mind when making your choice. Even if you have left the country, hospitals can be tenacious about getting their payment. Don't think that you can skip out on the bill. It's your expense. Pay it.

You should keep all your receipts in any case. Even if your insurer won't cover the services you have accepted, the costs may be tax-deductible. If there is a deductible on your policy or only some of your treatment is covered, the

---

TIP

Make Your Expenses Less Taxing

Keep all your medical receipts. If some of your expenses are not covered by your travel medical plan, you may be able to use them as a deduction on your income tax. And be sure and photocopy all your receipts before sending them to your insurance company ... just in case.

amount for which you are out of pocket may also be accepted as an income tax deduction. It is helpful if you can get your receipts issued in English or French. Don't waste any time sending in your claim. Many policies have a limit on how long you can wait before filing. If there isn't a claims form or instructions included in the policy you have purchased, call your insurer for details on how to get information to the company.

Before you go away, make sure you have access to enough cash or credit, just in case.

20. May I go ahead and call for help when I need it, or must I check with the insurance company?

If it is an emergency, get the help you need. Once the emergency has passed, you may need to call your insurer first before agreeing to any further treatments or procedures. Your insurer may have an agreement with a particular health care provider or may have restrictions on what procedures are covered that you should know about. If you are in crisis, you might need someone who can help you decide what care you really need before heading home.

21. Will they help me work through the system?

Some companies will and, unless you are visiting your birth country and are already familiar with the system, it can be very helpful. Some insurers have toll-free numbers linking you to representatives all over the world who can help arrange care and sort out details of your policy. Even people with second-language skills may have trouble navigating medical language outside their mother tongue. If you don't think you need that service, you may find a "fewer frills" company offering coverage with different options. That said, in some cases, you will be required to use a local assistance agency.

22. What if I disagree with my company's decision on what's required?

There are several steps you can take. Start by talking to your insurer, if you disagree with the company's decision. It is possible that the application wasn't clear, that someone made an error, or that second thoughts may make the claim go your way. If that doesn't work, you may wish to call the Canadian Life and Health Insurance Association (CLHIA). Information

Pack Your Documents

Remember to pack your provincial health care card, your travel insurance documents, and the emergency assistance number for your travel insurer.

counselors there can listen to your concerns and advise you on whether your complaint is worth pursuing. They may even be able to call the insurer on your behalf to help sort out any misunderstandings. CLHIA is a trade association representing most life and health insurance companies. It is not a licensing or government body and has no authority to tell a company what to do (see "Consumer Resources" in Appendix A for contact information).

In Ontario, each insurance company must have an ombudsperson on staff to handle conflicts. That person may be able to help with disputes outside Ontario as well. Although the ombudsperson position is not a requirement in other parts of Canada, there may be staff at the insurance company who handle customer complaints. If you are still not satisfied, go to the provincial government regulatory body (see Appendix A for contact information). In some cases, an ombudsperson or someone in a similar position will be available to assist. Again, however, this office can only use the powers of persuasion, although those powers are pretty substantial. If you are still not satisfied with the decision, your next step would be to take action through the courts.

Cancellation/baggage insurance

23. Do I need special insurance for my luggage, jewellery, computer?

If you have homeowners or tenants insurance (see chapter 2), your luggage is likely covered as "goods temporarily away from home." You will have to pay the deductible, however, and there are limits on the amount you can claim. You may want to start by determining with your insurance representative what you are already covered for.

In the case of jewellery, if the limit specified in your homeowners or tenants policy is not high enough to cover it adequately, you may need to buy an endorsement, or "add on," from your insurance representative to boost your coverage. If you are taking your laptop computer along on a working holiday, it won't be covered unless you have a separate business policy for it.

There is also a limit on what you can claim under a baggage insurance policy. You may be allowed up to $300 per lost item or up to about $2,000 for your entire set of luggage, for instance. Depending on how heavy you travel, $2,000 might not replace what you have in your suitcase. There could also be sub-limits for jewellery. Remember, those figures are based on the value of the average traveller's needs. If you aren't quite average, you should probably have a home or tenants insurance policy anyway (good advice even for average travellers).

Under a baggage insurance policy, you won't be covered for wear and tear of your goods or for damage caused by your own carelessness. Don't use your suitcase as a toboggan, for instance. Be careful how you pack, too. Many policies also won't cover antiques or fragile items that break in transit. Some plans do not cover sunglasses, false teeth, contact lenses, or tickets. You can probably guess why. Who hasn't lost one of those items or broken a treasured souvenir in the overhead bins? It just happens too often.

CAUTION

Baggage Insurance Won't Protect Valuables

Don't expect baggage insurance to cover your valuable jewellery or the laptop computer that you plan to take on a working holiday. Talk to the provider of your homeowners or tenants insurance to make sure those kinds of items are adequately covered.

Ask whether your policy includes coverage for delayed baggage. If your power suit lands at the Sydney airport and your business presentation is in Saskatoon, you may be able to buy appropriate clothing for your meeting.

24. Is cancellation insurance really insurance?

Insurance companies do underwrite cancellation policies, so yes, it is. But remember, bank tellers and travel agents are not trained insurance representatives and may not know all the ins and outs. Read the policy, ask questions, and call the company yourself if you don't understand.

Some policies might cover your costs if you cancel a trip because of a cancelled meeting, job transfer, or loss of employment. If the government issues an advisory recommending Canadians to not travel to your holiday destination, you would recoup your costs. Some weather conditions that prevent you from travelling may also be covered. If your travelling companion becomes ill or a family member dies, you would likely be able to claim the cost of your cancelled flight. However, if you were booked to travel to a dying relative's bedside and that relative died, you would not be covered for cancelling. Often, airlines will make provisions for compassionate cases. Since insurance companies look for other routes of payment first, they would take the airline's policy and top it up to the benefits you have purchased. You might also have access to meals or accommodation in case of an emergency or should you miss a departure because of bad weather or a vehicle breakdown. Don't expect it to be your choice of accommodations, by the way. This isn't your big chance to stay at the highest-priced hotel in town.

25. Are there conditions to cancellation insurance too?

Yes. You can't cancel a flight because you've changed your mind and expect to get your money back. You also can't cancel a ski vacation because you have a broken leg. As long as you are medically able to travel, you are on the hook for the cost. Cancellation insurance usually helps you recoup the cost of a trip if you have to cancel because you are suddenly unable to travel for medical reasons. The key word, again, is "suddenly." Restrictions for pre-existing conditions apply to cancellation insurance too. If you've been treated for a lung condition in the past three months, for example, and you take a turn for the worse the day before your flight, you won't be able to recoup your costs through cancellation insurance.

Remember that insurance is for the unexpected. If you have been seeking treatment for a problem, your insurer will figure the odds are good that that problem will prevent you from travelling. The risk is too high for the company to insure against.

26. Can I buy all this from my insurance provider?

You can purchase cancellation and baggage insurance from an insurance company or a travel agent. In fact, it is fairly simple to fill out the forms provided on the pamphlets available in pharmacies, banks, and travel agencies. You can buy insurance from some companies over the Internet. However, remember that filling out the form and sending a cheque does not mean that you are covered for everything.

Checklist

Top 10 questions to ask your insurance provider before you purchase your insurance.

1. What is not covered in the plan (including certain sports or other activities)?
2. Are there any other limitations (time period permitted for travel, age restriction, etc.)?
3. Is there a deductible? If so, how much?
4. How is a "pre-existing condition" defined? How do I determine if I have such a condition?
5. If I do have a pre-existing condition, can I still be covered for other, unrelated illnesses or injuries?

When You Have A Claim...

6. How do I make a claim?
7. Do I have to ask the insurance company before I receive treatment?
8. Will the claim be paid directly, or do I have to pay up front?
9. Will the plan pay for an air ambulance to transport me home in the case of a serious emergency?

10. Will the plan pay for someone to fly to my bedside if I am seriously ill or injured?

Keywords

Deductible	the portion of an insurance claim that you agree to pay out of pocket.
Pre-existing condition	an ailment or condition that you had diagnosed or for which you saw a physician or were taking treatment before you purchased your insurance policy.
Risk	the possibility of you developing a condition that will require you to file an insurance claim.
Travel health insurance	insurance that will help you pay for emergency medical care while you are away from your home province or country.
Underwriter	the company or individual within an insurance company who considers the risk to the company in accepting you as a policyholder.

appendix a:
consumer resources

Consumer Information

Canadian Association of Insurance and Financial Advisors
41 Lesmill Road
Don Mills, Ontario, M3B 2T3
Telephone: (416) 444-5251; toll-free: 1-800-563-5822; Fax: (416) 444-8031
E-mail: info@caifa.com; Web site: www.caifa.com

Canadian Coalition Against Insurance Fraud
151 Yonge Street, 18th Floor
Toronto, Ontario, M5C 2W7
Telephone: (416) 362-4550; Fax: (416) 362-4572
E-mail: webmaster@fraudcoalition.org; Web site: www.fraudcoalition.org

Canadian Life and Health Insurance Association
1 Queen Street East, Suite 1700
Toronto, Ontario, M5C 2X9
Telephone: (416) 777-2344; toll-free: 1-800-268-8099 (French: 1-800-361-8070); Fax: (416) 777-1895
E-mail (consumer assistance centre): CAC@clhia.ca;
Web site: www.clhia.ca

Canadian Life and Health Insurance Compensation Corporation
(CompCorp)
1 Queen Street East, Suite 1700
Toronto, Ontario, M5C 2X9
Telephone: (416) 359-2983; Fax: (416) 955-9688

Consumers' Association of Canada
Box 9300
Ottawa, Ontario, K1G 3T9
Telephone: (613) 238-2533; Fax: (613) 563-2254
E-mail: info@consumer.ca; Web site: www.consumer.ca

Consumers Council of Canada
14845-6 Yonge Street, Suite 149
Aurora, Ontario, L4G 6H8
Telephone: (905) 713-2740; Fax: (905) 713-2739
E-mail: ccc@tvo.org; Web site: www.consumerscouncil.com

Independent Life Insurance Brokers of Canada
Suite 301, 4263 Sherwoodtowne Blvd.
Mississauga, Ontario, L4Z 1Y5
Telephone: (905) 279-2727; toll-free: 1-888-654-3333; Fax: (905) 276-7295
E-mail: admin@lifebrokers.ca; Web site: www.lifebrokers.ca

Insurance Bureau of Canada
151 Yonge Street, Suite 1800
Toronto, Ontario, M5C 2W7
Telephone: (416) 362-2031; toll-free: 1-800-387-2880; Fax: (416) 361-5952
Web site: www.ibc.ca (see Web site for consumer information centres by province)

Insurance Canada (ConsumerInfo)
60 Columbia Way, Suite 300
Markham, Ontario, L3R 0C9
Telephone: (416) 591-0478; Fax: (905) 940-9445
E-mail: praskey@ibm.net; Web site: www.insurance-canada.ca

Medical Information Bureau
330 University Avenue, Suite 501
Toronto, Ontario, M5G 1R7
Telephone: (416) 597-0590
Web site: www.mib.com

Property and Casualty Insurance Compensation Corporation (PACICC)
20 Richmond Street East, Suite 210
Toronto, Ontario, M5C 2R9
Telephone: (416) 364-8677; Fax: (416) 364-5889

TRAC, a division of A. M. Best Canada Ltd.
600-133 Richmond Street West
Toronto, Ontario, M5H 2L3
Telephone: (416) 363-8266; toll-free: 1-800-263-8722;
Fax: (416) 363-2673
E-mail: insurance@trac.com; Web site: www.trac.com

Vehicle Information Centre of Canada
240 Duncan Mill Road, Suite 700
Don Mills, Ontario, M3B 1Z4
Telephone: (416) 445-1883; Fax: (416) 445-2183
E-mail: VICC@vicc.com; Web site: www.vicc.com

Licensing and Regulation
(see also "Superintendents of Insurance")

Alberta Insurance Council
901 Toronto Dominion Tower, Edmonton Centre
Edmonton, Alberta, T5J 2Z1
Telephone: (780) 421-4148; Fax: (780) 425-5745

Conseil des Assurances de Dommages
2020, rue University, Bureau 1919
Montreal, Quebec, H3A 2A5
Telephone: (514) 282-8765; toll-free (Quebec only): 1-800-667-7089
E-mail: info@conseilad.qc.ca; Web site: www.conseilad.qc.ca

Insurance Brokers Association of the Province of Quebec/L'Association des courtiers d'assurances de la province de Québec (ACAPQ)
500, rue Sherbrooke Ouest, 7e étage
Montréal, PQ, H3A 3C6
Telephone: (514) 842-2591; toll-free (Quebec): 1-800-361-7288;
Fax: (514) 842-3138
E-mail: acapq@videotron.ca

Insurance Council of British Columbia
300-1040 W. Georgia, P.O. Box 7
Vancouver, British Columbia, V6E 4H1
Telephone: (604) 688-0321; Fax: (604) 662-7767

Insurance Council of Manitoba
466-167 Lombard Avenue
Winnipeg, Manitoba, R3B 0T6
Telephone: (204) 988-6800; Fax: (204) 988-6801

Insurance Council of Saskatchewan
310-2631 28th Avenue
Regina, Saskatchewan, S4S 6X3
Telephone: (306) 347-0862; Fax: (306) 569-3018
E-mail: staff.ibas@ibas.sk.ca

Registered Insurance Brokers of Ontario (RIBO)
401 Bay Street, Suite 1200, P.O. Box 45
Toronto, Ontario, M5H 2Y4
Telephone: (416) 365-1900; toll-free: 1-800-265-3097; Fax: (416) 365-7664
Web site: www.ribo.com

Superintendents of Insurance

Federal
Office of the Superintendent of Financial Institutions
255 Albert Street, Kent Square, 16th Floor
Ottawa, Ontario, K1A 0H2
Telephone: (613) 990-7788; Fax: (613) 993-6782; toll-free (public complaints and inquiries assistance centre): 1-800-385-8647
E-mail: extcomm@osfi-bsif.gc.ca; Web site: www.osfi-bsif.gc.ca

Alberta
Alberta Treasury Dept.
Room 402, Terrace Building
9515-107 Street
Edmonton, Alberta, T5K 2C3
Telephone: (780) 442-1592; Fax: (780) 420-0752
Web site: www.treas.gov.ab.ca

British Columbia
Financial Institutions Commission
1050 West Pender Street, Suite 1900
Vancouver, British Columbia, V6E 3S7
Telephone: (604) 660-2947; Insurance complaints/inquiries:
(604) 660-2971 or (604) 775-2491; Fax: (604) 660-3170
Web site: www.fic.gov.bc.ca

Manitoba
Dept. of Consumer and Corporate Affairs
1115-405 Broadway
Winnipeg, Manitoba, R3C 3L6
Telephone: (204) 945-2542; toll-free: 1-800-282-8069; Fax: (204) 948-2268
E-mail: insurance@cca.gov.mb.ca; Web site: www.gov.mb.ca/cca

New Brunswick
Insurance Branch, Dept. of Justice
Room 477, 670 King Street, P.O. Box 6000
Fredericton, New Brunswick, E3B 5H1
Telephone: (506) 453-2512; Fax: (506) 453-7435

Newfoundland

Dept. of Government Services and Lands

Confederation Building, 2nd Floor, West Block, P.O. Box 8700

St. John's, Newfoundland, A1B 4J6

Telephone: (709) 729-2594; Fax: (709) 729-3205

E-mail: info@gov.nf.ca; Web site: www.gov.nf.ca/gsl

Northwest Territories

Dept. of Finance, Treasury Division, Government of the Northwest Territories

4922-48th Street, 3rd Floor, YK Centre, P.O. Box 1320

Yellowknife, Northwest Territories, X1A 2L9

Telephone: (867) 873-7308; Fax: (867) 873-0325

Web site: www.fin.gov.nt.ca

Nova Scotia

Dept. of Business and Consumer Services, Financial Institutions Division

1505 Barrington Street, 9th Floor South

Halifax, Nova Scotia, B3J 2X1

Telephone: (902) 424-6331; Fax: (902) 424-1298

E-mail: fininst@gov.ns.ca; Web site: www.gov.ns.ca/bacs/

Ontario

Financial Services Commission of Ontario

5160 Yonge Street, Box 85

North York, Ontario, M2N 6L9

Telephone: (416) 250-7250; toll-free: 1-800-668-0128; Fax: (416) 590-7070;

Fax insurance ombudsman: (416) 590-8480

Web site: www.fsco.gov.on.ca

Prince Edward Island

Dept. of Community Services & Attorney General

95 Rochford Street, P.O. Box 2000

Charlottetown, Prince Edward Island, C1A 7N8

Telephone: (902) 368-4564; Fax: (902) 368-5283

Web site: www.gov.pe.ca/caag/concorp/index.asp

Quebec

L'inspecteur général des institutions financières

800, place D'Youville, 9e étage

Québec (Qué.) G1R 4Y5

Telephone: (418) 528-9010; Fax: (418) 528-2791

E-mail: igif@igif.gouv.qc.ca; Web site: www.igif.gouv.qc.ca

Saskatchewan

Consumer Protection Branch

1871 Smith Street

Regina, Saskatchewan, S4P 3V7

Telephone: (306) 787-7881; toll-free: 1-888-374-4636;

Fax: (306) 787-9779

Yukon

Dept. of Justice J-6, Government of Yukon

P.O. Box 2703

Whitehorse, Yukon, Y1A 2C6

Telephone: (867) 667-5111; Fax: (867) 667-3609

E-mail: consumer@gov.yk.ca

appendix b:
consumer rights and responsibilities

In the past, members of the Consumers Council of Canada (CCC) have worked with consumer groups and the insurance industry to create a code of rights and responsibilities for both consumers and industry. The code clearly outlines what the Consumers Council believes your basic rights and responsibilities should be when you buy insurance.

Consumer Rights

The Right to Be Informed

- You have the right to information about insurance written in understandable language and printed in clear, easily readable type.
- You have the right to have policy provisions explained to you accurately before purchase.
- You have the right to be told in writing no less than 30 days in advance when the price and terms of your policy are to change and why.

The Right to Service

- You have the right to courteous service from a broker, agent, or insurance company when seeking to purchase insurance.
- You have the right to fair, prompt, and courteous attention to claims, policy changes, and enquiries.

The Right to Fair and Objective Guidance

- You have the right to fair and objective guidance to help you make an informed choice of the coverage that best meets your needs for quality protection, value, and personal service.

The Right to Redress

- In the event of a dispute with your insurance company, broker, or agent, you have the right to a clear explanation of their position.
- If you are not satisfied, you have the right to be informed of how to seek redress and how to contact the appropriate regulatory authority in order to make a formal complaint.

The Right to Privacy

- You have the right to privacy and confidentiality of all financial and personal information.

Consumer Responsibilities

The Responsibility to Be Informed

- You have the responsibility to question your broker, agent, or insurer, and to read the information they provide, so that you understand the concept of insurance and the details of your coverage.

The Responsibility to Help Control Losses

- You have the responsibility to minimize risk through practices such as safe driving and properly maintaining and safeguarding your vehicle and your home.

The Responsibility to Provide Accurate Information

- You have the responsibility to provide accurate information when you apply for insurance and to report claims accurately and promptly.

The Responsibility to Comply with Policy Provisions

- You have the responsibility to comply with the conditions of your insurance policies, including paying insurance premiums when they fall due and reporting all changes that may affect your insurance coverage.

The Responsibility to Report Fraudulent Practices

- You have the responsibility to minimize costs by reporting, to law enforcement authorities and your insurer, all attempts to defraud or circumvent the insurance system, recognizing that consumers ultimately pay for the settlement of all insurance claims.

The Consumers Council of Canada is an independent consumer organization helping business and government to understand and manage today's consumer issues. Its mandate is to improve the marketplace for consumers. To do that, the CCC consults with business and government and uses a network of people across Canada to answer surveys on topics of importance to consumers. The CCC has worked with consumer-focused companies to implement policies that benefit both consumers and business.

To find out more about the CCC and its consumer network, visit the Web site at www.consumerscouncil.com or e-mail the council: ccc@tvo.org

You can also write to the CCC:
Consumers Council of Canada
14845-6 Yonge Street, Suite 149
Aurora, ON L4G 6H8
Canada

glossary

Accident benefits   in automobile insurance, mandatory coverage that pays for your medical expenses and provides you with income replacement (up to a certain limit) if you are injured or killed in an accident, regardless of who was at fault.

Accidental death and dismemberment   coverage that provides a lump-sum payment to you or your survivors should an accident result in the loss of a limb, paralysis, or your death.

Actual cash value   the cost to repair or replace property, taking into consideration its age and condition at the time it was lost or damaged (replacement cost less depreciation).

Actuary   a person at an insurance company who prices future risks by applying mathematical models, so that the company will have enough money in reserve to pay future claims.

Adjuster   someone who investigates and settles claims for the insurance company. The adjuster may be an employee of the company, an independent contractor hired by the company or, less frequently, a public adjuster retained by the policyholder to represent his or her interests after a property loss.

Agent   a person who sells the products of one insurance company, and is employed by that company.

All Perils coverage   optional insurance that combines Collision and Comprehensive insurance on your automobile policy.

All risks policy   in home insurance, a policy that covers all losses except those specifically listed in the policy as "excluded" (not covered).

Annuity   in life insurance/estate planning, a contract that provides an income for a specified period of time, such as a number of years or for life.

At-fault accident   a car accident in which you are considered to be either completely or partially at fault, and which will go on your insurance record.

Beneficiary   the person named in a life insurance policy who receives the death benefit from that policy.

Benefits   the payment you would receive through your insurance plan.

Binder   a written or oral agreement that places insurance in force when it is not possible to issue a new policy immediately. It is subject to the premium and all the terms of the policy to be issued.

Broad-form policy   in home insurance, the intermediate level of coverage, covering all perils on the building except those that are specifically listed as exclusions in the policy, covers only "named perils" on the contents.

Broker   a person who sells the products of several different insurance companies, whether it be life, health, travel, disability, home, or car insurance.

Canadian Loss Experience Automobile Rating (CLEAR)   a system that rates cars for insurance purposes according to their previous claims record or "loss experience." It takes into account such factors as cost of repairs, frequency and severity of injury claims, and frequency of theft. Most insurers now use this system, rather than basing rates on the manufacturer's suggested list price, as was done in the past.

Cash value   in life insurance, the part of a permanent insurance policy that builds up over time. The policyholder may choose to cash in the policy if he/she no longer requires the life coverage, but this forfeits the death benefit.

Claim   a person's request for payment by an insurer for a loss covered under an insurance policy.

Claims handler/examiner   the employee at the insurance company who looks after your claim. This person is supervised by a claims manager.

CLEAR   *see* Canadian Loss Experience Automobile Rating

Collision insurance   optional insurance that pays to have your car repaired or replaced when it is damaged in a collision with another car or object (but not with an animal), or by rolling over.

Comprehensive insurance   optional insurance that pays to replace loss or damage to your car other than that caused by collision or upset; for example, damage caused by falling or flying objects, flood, earthquake, fire, theft, vandalism, and collision with animals. A comprehensive policy, on the other hand, is the most extensive, and expensive, type of home policy, covering everything that isn't specifically excluded on both the building and contents.

Convertibility   the ability to change from one type of life insurance policy to another, without having to give evidence of insurability.

Critical illness insurance   coverage that provides money should you become seriously ill with cancer, heart disease, stroke, or other specified illnesses. It pays a lump sum that you can spend on whatever you want.

Customer service representative (CSR)   an employee at an insurance brokerage or insurance company who assists in handling requests from clients. This person is not the same as an insurance broker, who must be licensed.

Death benefit   the money paid out on a life insurance policy after a death claim is approved.

Deductible   the portion of the loss that you agree to pay out of your pocket, before the insurance company pays the amount it is obligated to cover. For example, if your claim is for $1,500 and your deductible is $500, you pay $500 and the insurance company pays $1,000.

Depreciation   reduction in the value of property due to age and use. This is taken into account when the insurance company pays you Actual Cash Value for your claim.

Direct-response insurer   an insurance company whose representatives sell only that company's products, directly over the telephone.

Direct seller. *see* Direct-response insurer

Direct writer an insurance company that employs its own agents, as opposed to brokers, to sell its products. Agents of direct writers work from a number of branch offices, unlike direct-response insurers, which operate from one location known as a call centre.

Disability the inability, due to illness or injury, to continue working.

Endorsement an amendment or "extra" that can be added to your policy to beef up your coverage; also called a "rider" or "floater."

Exclusion specific conditions or circumstances listed in the policy that are not covered by the policy.

Extended health care coverage for care and devices beyond what's provided for in your provincial health plan: physical and psychological therapies provided by chiropractors, physiotherapists, speech pathologists, etc.; physical devices such as hearing aids, prosthetic appliances and medical equipment; and home care and nursing.

Facility Association in automobile insurance, an industry-sponsored pool "of last resort" for high-risk drivers who can't get insurance with a regular company. Premiums are much higher than in the regular insurance market.

First-party claim a claim you make to your own insurance company.

Floater additional coverage for movable items, like jewellery or antiques, beyond what's included in the basic home policy. Also called a "rider" or "endorsement."

Group insurance insurance that is offered through your workplace, alumni association, professional association, union, or other group affiliation.

Guaranteed renewal a promise by the insurance company that a life insurance policy will be renewed without penalty or a medical examination after the term has expired. The renewal rate can also be guaranteed.

Health insurance insurance that will help you pay for medication, as well as vision, dental, or other health care.

Indemnification compensation to the victim of a loss, by payment, repair, or replacement.

Insured the person or organization covered by an insurance policy.

Level premium in life insurance, a premium that remains unchanged throughout the life of a policy.

Liability a legally enforceable financial obligation. Liability insurance pays the losses of other people when you are legally responsible for an accident in which you have unintentionally injured another person or damaged his or her property.

Living benefits. *see* Viatical settlement

Long-term care insurance coverage that provides for health care on a long-term basis, at home or in a care facility.

Loss an event that causes an insurance claim. The loss could result from fire, theft, automobile accident, or many other causes.

Named perils policy   in home insurance, the most basic type of policy, covering only those perils that are specifically listed—or named—in the policy, for both the building and its contents.

No-fault insurance   in automobile insurance, a system whereby accident victims collect benefits for medical expenses and lost income from their own insurance company, regardless of who was at fault.

Occurrence   an accident that results in bodily injury or property damage during the period of an insurance policy.

Participating insurance   in life insurance, a policy in which the policy owner is entitled to receive dividends.

Peril   the cause of loss or damage, such as fire or theft.

Permanent insurance   life insurance that covers you for your whole life; usually has an investment element, as well as a cash value option that allows you, after several years, to cash in the policy (at the same time giving up the death benefit). Whole life and universal life insurance are types of permanent insurance.

Personal lines insurance   insurance, usually home or car, for individuals, as opposed to commercial lines insurance for businesses.

Personal property   your possessions; the contents of your house, apartment, or condominium.

Policy   the legal document issued by the insurance company that outlines the terms and conditions of the insurance.

Policyholder   the person who buys the insurance and owns the policy.

Pre-existing condition   an ailment or condition that you have had diagnosed or for which you have seen a physician or are taking treatment before you purchased your insurance policy.

Premium   the payment required to keep your insurance policy in force.

Proof of loss   documents that you give to your insurer to support your request for payment of a claim; for example, appraisals, receipts, physician's report, etc.

Property insurance   the insurance on your house and its contents, as well as liability protection. There are also special property insurance packages for renters and condominium unit owners.

Replacement cost insurance   insurance that covers the cost of replacing an item at today's prices, without taking depreciation into account. In order to receive replacement cost, you must replace the original item with one that is as close as possible in functionality and quality.

Rider   optional protection purchased as an extra on an insurance policy, such as the "accidental death benefit"; also called an "endorsement."

Risk   the chance of a loss; also used to refer to the person or property covered by the policy; also used to refer to the possibility of you making a claim.

Risk factors   variables that insurance companies take into account when pricing your policy. For example, how far you drive your car each day, whether you live in the city or the country, how close your house is to a fire hydrant, etc.

Salvage usually used to describe what's left of a vehicle that has been damaged beyond repair in an accident (a "write-off"). Once you accept payment for your damaged car, the salvage becomes the property of the insurance company.

Scheduling listing any valuable items, like jewellery, separately on your policy, so you can insure each article for a specific amount beyond the normal limits of your policy.

Specified perils coverage in automobile insurance, optional insurance against loss or damage caused by specific perils listed on the policy. Similar to, but not as broad as, Comprehensive auto insurance.

Subrogation the process in which an insurance company pays a claim, and then recovers all or part of that amount from the person who actually caused the loss.

Term insurance a life insurance policy issued for a specific period, say, 5, 10, 20, or even 100 years.

Third-party claim a claim made by one person against another person's insurance company.

Travel health insurance insurance that will help you pay for emergency medical care while you are away from your home country.

Underwriter the company or individual within an insurance company who considers the risk to the company in accepting someone as a policyholder.

Underwriting the process of selecting risks for insurance, and determining how much to charge to insure these risks.

Uninsured motorist coverage car insurance that pays for injury to you or your passengers caused by an uninsured or a hit-and-run driver.

Universal life insurance a type of policy that combines term insurance with flexible premiums and a separate savings program directed, to some extent, by the policyholder.

Viatical settlement payment of a portion of the proceeds from life insurance to an insured who is terminally ill; also referred to as "living benefits."

Whole life insurance a life insurance policy with a cash value component that protects for one's entire life.

index